CONTEÚDO DIGITAL PARA ALUNOS

Cadastre-se e transforme seus estudos em uma experiência única de aprendizado:

1 Escaneie o QR Code para acessar a página de cadastro.

2 Complete-a com seus dados pessoais e as informações de sua escola.

3 Adicione ao cadastro o código do aluno, que garante a exclusividade de acesso.

9295383A2719032

Agora, acesse:
www.editoradobrasil.com.br/leb
e aprenda de forma inovadora
e diferente! :D

Lembre-se de que esse código, pessoal e intransferível, é válido por um ano. Guarde-o com cuidado, pois é a única maneira de você utilizar os conteúdos da plataforma.

MARIANA CARDIERI MENDONÇA
- Professora de inglês da rede particular de ensino
- Diplomada com *First Certificate in English*, pela Cambridge e pelo Toefl

PAULA SCHWARTZ CALDERARI
- Mestre em Ensino de Inglês pela *University of Western Ontario*
- Pós-graduada em Gestão das Organizações Educacionais pela *FAE Business School*
- Instrutora de Inglês Acadêmico na *University of Western Ontario*

APOEMA
INGLÊS
9

1ª edição
São Paulo, 2018

Dados Internacionais de Catalogação na Publicação (CIP)
(Câmara Brasileira do Livro, SP, Brasil)

Mendonça, Mariana Cardieri
  Apoema: inglês 9 / Mariana Cardieri Mendonça, Paula Schwartz Calderari. – 1. ed. – São Paulo: Editora do Brasil, 2018. – (Coleção apoema)

  ISBN 978-85-10-06956-4 (aluno)
  ISBN 978-85-10-06957-1 (professor)

  1. Inglês (Ensino fundamental) I. Calderari, Paula Schwartz. II. Título. III. Série.

18-20643   CDD-372.652

Índices para catálogo sistemático:
1. Inglês: Ensino fundamental 372.652
Maria Alice Ferreira – Bibliotecária – CRB-8/7964

1ª edição / 2ª impressão, 2020
Impresso na BMF Gráfica e Editora

Rua Conselheiro Nébias, 887
São Paulo, SP – CEP 01203-001
Fone: +55 11 3226-0211
www.editoradobrasil.com.br

© Editora do Brasil S.A., 2018
Todos os direitos reservados

Direção-geral: Vicente Tortamano Avanso

Direção editorial: Felipe Ramos Poletti
Gerência editorial: Erika Caldin
Supervisão de arte e editoração: Cida Alves
Supervisão de revisão: Dora Helena Feres
Supervisão de iconografia: Léo Burgos
Supervisão de Digital: Ethel Shuña Queiroz
Supervisão de controle de processos editoriais: Marta Dias Portero
Supervisão de direitos autorais: Marilisa Bertolone Mendes

Supervisão editorial: Carla Felix Lopes
Edição: Amanda Leal e Monika Kratzer
Assistência editorial: Ana Okada e Juliana Pavoni
Auxiliar editorial: Beatriz Villanueva
Coordenação de revisão: Otacilio Palareti
Copidesque: Claudia Cantarin e Evelyn Zaidan Porting
Revisão: Beatriz Moreira Guedes
Pesquisa iconográfica: Isabela Meneses
Assistência de arte: Samira de Souza
Design gráfico: Anexo Produção Editorial
Imagem da capa: Mauro77photo/Dreamstime.com
Capa: Megalo Design
Ilustrações: Christiane S Messias, Cristiane Viana, Danillo Souza, DKO Estúdio, João P. Mazzoco, Kau Bispo e Marcos Guilherme
Coordenação de editoração eletrônica: Abdonildo José de Lima Santos
Editoração eletrônica: Daniel Campos Souza, Flávia Jaconis, José Anderson Campos, Maira Spilack, Marcos Gubiotti, Ricardo Brito, Sérgio Rocha e Talita Lima
Licenciamentos de textos: Cinthya Utiyama, Jennifer Xavier, Paula Harue Tozaki e Renata Garbellini
Produção fonográfica: Jennifer Xavier e Cinthya Utiyama
Controle de processos editoriais: Bruna Alves, Carlos Nunes, Jefferson Galdino, Rafael Machado e Stephanie Paparella

HEY, STUDENT! WELCOME TO APOEMA!

A língua inglesa está cada vez mais presente nos nossos dias, seja na internet, na escola ou no trabalho. Tiramos *selfies* para postar nas redes sociais, levamos o *dog* para passear e fazemos a *homework* da escola, assistimos aos *youtubers* favoritos, vemos nossas séries e ouvimos nossas músicas em plataformas de *streaming* entre tantas outras coisas.

O conhecimento desta língua estrangeira é essencial para que possamos conhecer novos mundos, ampliar nossos horizontes e estarmos conectados com o que acontece ao nosso redor e no mundo. Por isso, é importante, e também gratificante, conhecer essa língua que conecta o mundo todo, compreender as culturas das quais ela faz parte.

Pensando nisso, nesta nova versão do **Apoema**, palavra da língua tupi que significa "aquele que vê mais longe", nosso objetivo não é apenas ensinar a língua estrangeira, mas também apresentar os diferentes lugares e culturas em que o inglês é o idioma nativo.

Nossa proposta é apresentar a língua inglesa de forma dinâmica, atual, interessante e ligada ao mundo real para que você possa usá-la para se comunicar, entendê-la e escrevê-la de forma fluente, interagindo com o mundo e expandindo seus horizontes, ou seja, vendo mais longe.

LET'S GET DOWN TO WORK!

Rawpixel.com/Shutterstock.com

SUMÁRIO

Unit 1 – What will your future be like?

Chapter 1	**Let's practice** – Life plans	8
	Let's listen n' speak – Life plans	10
	Language piece – Conjunctions	10
Chapter 2	**Let's practice** – Future simple tense (will)	11
	Language piece – Future: will	11
	Vocabulary hint – The individual sound of the contraction	12
	Let's listen n' speak – Future tense (will)	13
Chapter 3	**Let's read n' write** – Article – Generation Z, unlike any other	15
Chapter 4	**Tying in** – Generations across the 20TH century	18
	Project – Which generation am I?	19

Unit 2 – What are you going to choose?

Chapter 1	**Let's practice** – Future plans	22
	Let's listen n' speak – Decision making	24
Chapter 2	**Let's practice** – Future tense – (be) going to	25
	Language piece – Future: be going to	26
	Vocabulary hint – Going to contraction	27
	Let's listen n' speak – Future tense – (be) going to	28
Chapter 3	**Let's read n' write** – Personal Essay – My future	29
Chapter 4	**Citizenship moment** – Elections 101	32
	Project – Political systems	33

Review	34 e 35
Do not forget	36
Overcoming challenges	37

Unit 3 – How are they going to travel?

Chapter 1	**Let's practice** – Means of transportation	40
	– Adjectives to describe means of transportation	40
	Let's listen n' speak – Travel vocabulary	41
Chapter 2	**Let's practice** – Embedded questions x Direct questions	43
	Language piece – Embedded question	43
	Let's listen n' speak – Embedded questions x Direct questions	44
	Let's practice – Will × (Be) going to	45
	Language piece – Will × (Be) going to	45
	Vocabulary hint – Linking sounds – Consonant To Vowel (CTV)	45
Chapter 3	**Let's read n' write** – Postcards	47
Chapter 4	**Tying in** – The evolution of transportation	50
	Let's practice	51
	Project – Brazil transportation technology	51

Unit 4 – Should we be more careful?

Chapter 1	**Let's practice** – Abbreviations (internet language)	54
	Let's listen n' speak – Internet safety	56
Chapter 2	**Let's practice** – Giving advice – modal verbs	57
	Language piece – Modal verbs	58
	Vocabulary hint – Modal verbs	58
	Let's listen n' speak – Expressing obligation or necessity – modal verbs	60
Chapter 3	**Let's read n' write** – Social media profile	61
Chapter 4	**Citizenship moment** – Things to come: A timeline of future technology	64
	Let's practice	65
	Project – Technological device timeline	65

Review	66 e 67
Do not forget	68
Overcoming challenges	69

Unit 5 – Have you played as a kid?

Chapter 1	**Let's practice** – Childhood games	**72**
	Let's listen n' speak – Childhood memories	**74**
Chapter 2	**Let's practice** – Past perfect tense	**75**
	Language piece – Past perfect	**75**
	Vocabulary hint – Past perfect	**76**
	Let's listen n' speak – Baseball bat	**78**
Chapter 3	**Let's read n' write** – Timeline – 20th-Century Toys and Games Timeline	**79**
Chapter 4	**Citzenship moment** – Rights of the child	**82**
	Let's practice	**83**
	Project – Research: ECA	**83**

Unit 6 – How much have our lives changed?

Chapter 1	**Let's practice** – Technological devices	**86**
	– Means of communication	**86**
	Let's listen n' speak – Past and present	**88**
Chapter 2	**Let's practice** – Passive voice – present and past tense	**89**
	Language piece – Passive voice	**90**
	Vocabulary hint – Passive voice	**91**
	Let's listen n' speak – Passive voice – present and past tense	**92**
Chapter 3	**Let's read n' write** – Disruptive Technology	**93**
Chapter 4	**Tying in** – Cross Cultural Awareness and Communication	**96**
	Let's practice	**97**
	Project – Classroom communication system	**97**

Review	**98 e 99**
Do not forget	**100**
Overcoming challenges	**101**

Unit 7 – What if the stories were true?

Chapter 1	**Let's practice** – Mythological and Fantastic figures	**104**
	Let's listen n' speak – Myths	**106**
Chapter 2	**Let's practice** – First conditional	**107**
	Language piece – First conditional	**107**
	Vocabulary hint – First conditional – order of clauses	**108**
	Let's listen n' speak – First conditional	**110**
Chapter 3	**Let's read n' write** – King Midas Script	**111**
Chapter 4	**Tying in** – Brazil – Mythology and Folklore	**114**
	Let's practice	**115**
	Project – World's best known Mythological Figures	**115**

Unit 8 – What if we took better care of nature?

Chapter 1	**Let's practice** – Recyclable and non recyclables items	**118**
	Let's listen n' speak – Natural resources	**120**
Chapter 2	**Let's practice** – Second conditional	**121**
	Language piece – Second conditional	**121**
	– Third conditional	**122**
	Let's listen n' speak	**123**
	Language piece – Intonation	**124**
Chapter 3	**Let's read n' write** – News – What happens when the world's resources run out?	**125**
Chapter 4	**Citzenship moment** – Reduce, Reuse, Recycle	**128**
	Let's practice – Expressions	**129**
	Project – Expressions	**129**

Review	**130 e 131**
Do not forget	**132**
Overcoming challenges	**133**

Workbook	**134 a 149**
Expert's Point I	**150 a 153**
I. A Year Abroad	**150 e 151**
II. Your guide to green holidays	**152 e 153**

Focus on culture	**154 a 157**
I. Internet Safety	**154 e 155**
II. Greenhouse Effect and Global Warming	**156 e 157**
Language Court	**158 a 172**
Glossary	**173**

UNIT 1
WHAT WILL YOUR FUTURE BE LIKE?

||| Get ready |||

1 What do these scenes represent? Choose the best description from the options in the box.

> apply for college • get a job • go abroad
> buy a house • get married • graduate

2 Now, use the expressions in exercise 1 to complete the following sentences.

a) I will _____ after high school.

b) Susan will _____ from college in two years.

c) Kevin plans to _____ for a year after college.

d) Mary hopes she _____ before graduating.

e) I plan to _____ of my own in ten years.

f) Eleonor and Connor will _____ on November 13th.

3 What about your plans for the future? Team up and exchange plans with your classmates.

CHAPTER 1

Let's practice

1 Some years from now. Read what these teenagers imagine about their future and answer the questions.

The future

Pedro, Cuiabá, Brazil

After I finish **high school** I'll probably study biology because I really enjoy nature matters. I'll **definitely** apply for some public universities. I plan on traveling to some exotic places to find out more about different ecosystems.

Agnes, Athenas, Greece

I love designing spaces so I'll get into a good design college course and when I graduate I plan to get a job at a big design company and move to another country, like USA.

Min-seo, Seoul, South Korea

I really like taking care of people, so I think I'll study medicine, so I'll apply for a good **college**. I plan to become a surgeon and help lots of people.

Zaki, Cape Town, South Africa

I think a good education is essential, so I'll definitely apply to a good college and study **Law**. I plan on helping a lot of people who need, but cannot pay for it.

GLOSSARY

College: faculdade.
Definitely: definitivamente.
High school: Ensino Médio.
Law: Direito.

a) What topic are they talking about?

- ( ) Education.
- ( ) Relationships.
- ( ) Carreer.

b) Who will study this? Match.

- Design
- Law
- Medicine
- Biology

- Pedro
- Agnes
- Min-seo
- Zaki

c) Why do they want to pursue these careers?

- Agnes _____

_____

- Min-seo _____

_____

- Pedro _____

_____

- Zaki _____

2 **What about you? What will your life be like in a decade? Complete the following sentences about your future.**

a) I think I will... _____.

b) I don't think I will... _____.

c) I probably will... _____.

d) I definitely will... _____.

3 **What do you imagine your future will be like in 2050? Use the questions below to write a short composition about it on your notebook.**

- How old will you be in 2050?
- Where will you live: in the country, in the city, at the beach or in the mountains?
- Will you live in a house or in an apartment?
- What will your occupation be?

- Will you be successful?
- Will you be married?
- Will you have children?
- Will you have possessions? Which ones?
- Will you help other people?

9

1. Listen to a chat between some friends and answer the following questions.

a) Where will Thomas and Oliver apply for? Why is it difficult?

_____

b) What do Thomas and Oliver plan to do in order to get in the MIT?

_____

c) What will Thomas and Oliver do today?

_____

d) Why do Thomas and Oliver need to plan their schedule wisely?

_____

e) Will Kate join in the planning discussion?

_____

2. Listen again and complete the sentences with so or because.

a) It will demand a lot of hard working _____ there is a lot of competition.

b) I'll just grab a pen and some paper _____ we can start the planning.

3. Pair up and exchange opinions about the following topics.

- What do you hope to do in your life?
- What does the future hold for you?
- Where do you plan on going in the future?
- What is your lifetime dream?

LANGUAGE PIECE

Conjunctions

Because   expresses the reason for something.

So   expresses the result of something.

Let's practice

1 Circle the correct option.

a) Let's stay home Friday night. I think it _____ be cold. (will / won't)

b) Giorgio is away, so he _____ be at the meeting with us today. (will / won't)

c) They _____ apply for a foreign college. (will / won't)

d) My teacher _____ give a test first thing tomorrow. (will / won't)

e) We _____ buy this product, it's too expensive. (will / won't)

f) Take an umbrella. It _____ rain this afternoon. (will / won't)

g) Karen _____ scream! She is not afraid of spiders. (will / won't)

h) The ice storm is terrible. Accidents _____ happen because of it. (will / won't)

i) They _____ arrive early because their practice ends late today. (will / won't)

2 Decide if the sentence is **C** (correct) or **I** (incorrect).

a) ( ) I think I become a pediatrician.
b) ( ) Suzana will not travels this year.
c) ( ) He will not be home until 9 p.m.
d) ( ) You will making a good journalist.
e) ( ) We won't not take more than 10 minutes, I promise.
f) ( ) The train will leave at 11:45.
g) ( ) They will not traveled to London on Friday evening.

3 Rewrite the incorrect sentences from the previous exercise to make them right.

_____
_____
_____
_____

LANGUAGE PIECE

Future: will
Affirmative:
Subject pronoun + will + verb (infinitive) + complement.
They will be mathematicians.
Negative:
Subject pronoun + will + not + verb (infinitive) + complement.
I will not (won't) eat this sandwich.

11

4 Reorder the words to form interrogative sentences.

a) Chris – here – Friday – after – will – be

_____

b) take – we – to – the – airport – will – taxi – later – a – today

_____

c) meeting – our – will – at – 8 a.m. – happen

_____

d) too – long – they – to – get – will – take – back

_____

e) the – interview – be – long – will

_____

> **LANGUAGE PIECE**
>
> **Future: will**
> **Interrogative:**
> Will + subject pronoun + verb (infinitive) + complement + ?
> Will she be a famous actress?

5 Write questions to the following answers.

a) _____
Bob will move abroad next month.

b) _____
Yes, they will get married next year.

c) _____
Noah will retire next year.

d) _____
No, not now. The test will begin after the break.

e) _____
Liz will buy a studio in two weeks.

>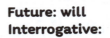
>
> **Vocabulary hint**
> **Will sounds**
> The individual sound of the contraction:
>
> I will → I'll
> You will → You'll
> He will → He'll
> She will → She'll
> It will → It'll
> We will → We'll
> They will → They'll
>
> **In a sentence:**
> I'll check later.
> She'll see you later today.
> They'll travel tomorrow.

6 Write questions with the prompts below using **will** and answer them to be true for you.

a) go to college _____

b) travel abroad _____

c) get a dream job _____

Let's listen n' speak

1 Listen to Adrian and Joan and write **T** (true) or **F** (false).

a) ◯ Adrian is talking to a stranger.

b) ◯ Adrian is Greek.

c) ◯ Adrian is a fast reader.

d) ◯ Adrian's father wants him to rest this afternoon.

e) ◯ Joan advises Adrian's father on what to do.

2 Label the images as it follows.

> It already happened. • It is happening. • It will probably happen.

a) _____

d) _____

b) _____

e) _____

c) _____

f) _____

Ilustrações: Kau Bispo

3 Answer the following questions about the chat between Adrian and Joan.

a) How many books will Adrian take home today?

_____

b) What Adrian needs to do because his dad asked him to?

_____

c) Adrian mentioned Joan is good at something. What is that?

_____

d) What will Adrian probably do this afternoon?

_____

4 Listen to the dialogue again and complete the sentences with the missing words.

a) Good morning, Joan. I finished the one you recommended on Monday, _____ here I am again! Returning this one and taking this one.

b) Well, I will read it _____ I can dodge my dad.

c) No, it's _____ he's been asking me to take care of the yard since Friday. But honestly,

I am tired, _____ I just want to be quiet by the pool, sunbathe and enjoy my reading.

d) _____ you will need to negotiate with him. _____ I can be nosy, say you need to rest this afternoon and that you will mow the lawn tomorrow.

e) Hmm, that sounds fair and easy. You are good at talking to people, _____ I guess I will follow your advice. Thanks a lot, Joan!

5 Pair up and choose some prompts from the box to make questions to one another. Use the conjunctions **so**, **because**, **if**, **then**, and time words like **tonight**, **tomorrow**, **on the weekend** etc.

- go to the beach
- have a party tonight
- go shopping
- get a new pet
- read
- organize my bedroom
- call my grandparents
- study
- cook

LANGUAGE PIECE

Conjunctions

Because	expresses the reason for something.
So	expresses the result of something.
If	expresses an assumption or condition for something to happen.
Then	expresses a consequence, or result of something.

Chapter 3 — Let's read n' write

YOUTH

Generation Z – unlike any other

Who are the "Generation Z"? The generation after the called Millennials has started around mid-1990s and its members are ready to become the dominant **youth** influencers of tomorrow.

Generation Z is being considered a more **conscientious**, hard-working, anxious and **mindful** of the future than the previous ones. Being the first generation raised in the era of smartphones, they are intrinsically connected to technology and considered the first true digital natives. "The average teen spends about two and a half hours a day on electronic devices," wrote Jean Twenge, a psychologist in an Atlantic article.

This generation is able to process information faster than any other generation, consequently its attention **spans** might be significantly shorter than the previous generation. However, this generation can be better multi taskers, being able to quickly and efficiently **shift** from task to task with multiple distractions around.

According to the findings of a survey done by the psychologists Jean Twenge and Heejung Park, this generation present itself as less **reckless** and more socially isolated than the previous ones. They are being **perceived** as a generation with no hurry to grow up.

Generation Z has been considered more cautious with privacy issues and the **pursue** of **sensible** careers.

According to the previous mentioned research, around only 55 percent of teenagers have already worked for a paying job. They **seek** for being more pragmatists than idealists, and for more independent work environments. As reported by Deep Patel, a marketing strategist, "the newly developing high tech and highly networked world has resulted in an entire generation thinking and acting more **entrepreneurially**."

Based on: *Move over, millennials, here comes generations Z*. Available at: <www.nytimes.com/2015/09/20/fashion/move-over-millennials-here-comes-generation-z.html>; *A 40-year study of teens finds Generation Z is unlike any past generation – here's what they're all about*. Available at: <www.businessinsider.com/generation-z-teens-what-theyre-all-about-2017-9#they-spend-a-lot-of-time-on-their-phones-7>; *8 key differences between Gen Z and Millennials*. Available at: <https://www.huffingtonpost.com/george-beall/8-key-differences-between_b_12814200.html>. Access: Aug. 2018.

GLOSSARY

Conscientious: consciente.
Entrepreneurially: de maneira empreendedora.
Mindful: atento.
Perceived (to perceive): percebidos (perceber).
Pursue (to pursue): buscar, ir atrás de.
Reckless: imprudente.
Seek (to seek): procuram (procurar).
Sensible: sensato.
Shift: mudança.
Spans: períodos.
Youth: juventude.

1 **Read the previous article and answer the following questions.**

a) What is the article about?

_____

b) How is the prior generation to Generation Z called?

_____

c) When is it believed Generation Z people began to be born?

_____

d) What are the differences between Generation Z and its prior generations?

_____

_____

e) Why is Generation Z considered the first true digital natives?

_____

_____

f) According to whom? Match the sentences to the specialist who said them according to the text.

Deep Patel, marketing strategist • Jean Twenge, psychologist

"The average teen spends about two and a half hours a day on electronic devices."

_____

_____

"The newly developing high tech and highly networked world has resulted in an entire generation thinking and acting more entrepreneurially."

_____

_____

g) Check all Generation Z's characteristics.

- ◯ multi-taskers
- ◯ easily dispersed
- ◯ more carefree
- ◯ more cautious

- ◯ more sociable
- ◯ more socially isolated
- ◯ more autonomous
- ◯ more reliant

- ◯ more reserved
- ◯ pragmatic
- ◯ idealistic
- ◯ entrepreneurial

2 Think about the text and its characteristics and answer the questions.

a) What does the text aim to?
_____

b) What kind of language is used in it?
_____

c) What elements are part of this type of text?
_____
_____

d) What kind of text is an article? What information does it bring? Check all that applies.
- ◯ Empirical facts.
- ◯ Data.
- ◯ Descriptive.
- ◯ Informative.
- ◯ Hypothetical facts.
- ◯ Persuasive.

e) Where can texts like this be found?
_____
_____

3 Now write an informative article upon the differences between Millennials and Generation Z. Use the following briefing to help you out.

- Research about the characteristics of Millennials and Generation Z.
- Make a chart with the main contrastive aspects.
- Gather data from reliable sources by trustworthy authorities on the subject.
- Write a draft and make a peer evaluation of it with your classmates.
- Write a new version of the article, making all the necessary adjustments.
- Hand your article to your teacher.

CHAPTER 4 — ||| Tying in |||

GENERATIONS ACROSS THE 20TH CENTURY

Generation is a group of people born and raised around the same time and who exhibit similar characteristics, preferences, and values over their lifetimes once they've experienced similar **trends** at approximately the same life stage and through similar channels.

G.I. GENERATION/GREATEST GENERATION
BORN 1901 TO 1924

Archetype: HERO – born and raised during a time of individual pragmatism, **self-reliant**, and nationalism.
Reputation: **Selfless**, rational, prudent, faithful and competent.

SILENT/TRADITIONALISTS
BORN 1945 AND BEFORE

Archetype: ARTIST – born and raised during a time when great worldly **perils boil off** complexity of life and public consensus aggressive institutions and personal sacrifice **prevail**.
Reputation: Rational, conservative, patriotic, patient, practical, respectful and team player.

BABY BOOMERS
BORN 1946 TO 1964

Archetype: PROPHET – born and raised during a time of rejuvenated community life and new societal order.
Reputation: Conscientious, **resolute**, optimistic, individualistic, ambitious and workaholic.

MILLENNIALS/GENERATION Y
BORN 1977 TO 1995

Archetype: HERO – born and raised during a time of individual pragmatism, self-reliance and nationalism.
Reputation: Hopeful, optimistic, impatient, individualistic yet group-oriented and **tech-savvy**.

GENERATION X
BORN 1965 TO 1976

Archetype: NOMAD – born and raised during a time of social ideals and spiritual agendas with the break out against established institutional order.
Reputation: Independent, self-reliant, skeptical and risk-taker.

GENERATION Z /IGEN/CENTENNIALS/HOMELANDERS
BORN 1996 AND LATER

Archetype: ARTIST – born and raised during a time when great worldly perils boil off complexity of life and public consensus aggressive institutions, and personal sacrifice prevail.
Reputation: Highly technological, anxious, short attention span, multi-tasker, **entrepreneurial**, individualistic, collaborative, and creative.

GLOSSARY

Boil off (to boil off): fervem (ferver).
Entrepreneurial: empreendedor.
Perils: perigos.
Prevail (to prevail): prevalecem (prevalecer).
Resolute: resoluto.
Selfless: altruísta.
Self-reliant: autossuficiente.
Tech-savvy: pessoa que entende de tecnologia.
Trends: tendências.

Based on: *Generations Timeline*. Available at: <http://afterthemillennials.com/generations-archetype-turnings/>; *Generational Breakdown: Info about all of the generations*. Available at: <http://genhq.com/faq-info-about-generations/>; Timeline: American Generations since 20th Century. Available at: <http://projects.scpr.org/timelines/american-generations-timeline/>; Here's which generation you're part of based on your birth year - and why those distinctions exist. Available at: <www.businessinsider.com/generation-you-are-in-by-birth-year-millennial-gen-x-baby-boomer-2018-3>; *Generational Names in the United States*. Available at: <www.thoughtco.com/names-of-generations-1435472>; *Generational Archetypes*. Available at: <www.lifecourse.com/about/method/generational-archetypes.html>. Access: Aug. 2018.

Let's practice

 1 What generation are they from? Read their descriptions and match with the most suitable generation according to the infographic.

> Baby Boomers • G.I. Generation • Generation X
> Generation Z • Millennials • Silent Generation

a)  I have worked very hard since very young. For me it is very important to be successful and have a comfortable life.

d)  I'm an independent woman who works hard to make my own business successful.

b)  I've seen many wars and a lot of society changes, that's the reason why I believe we should be more helpful with each other.

e)  I get bored too fast. I like to watch a movie on TV while I chat with my social media friends and play an interactive game on my smartphone.

c)  I've worked hard in the same company for almost my whole life. I like people who are engaged in working together and having clear-cut responsibilities.

f)  I believe we can change the world and that our individualities are our best characteristics. Technology is what will bring us together for good.

PROJECT

Which generation am I?
Research about your generation and write all the characteristics you believe you have and think of reasons that support your opinion. Exchange ideas with your classmates.

EXPLORING

My life, My plan
- <www.beststart.org/resources/preconception/MLMP_14MY01_Final.pdf>

Teen Game Plan
- <www.safeteens.org/teen-game-plan/>

UNIT 2
WHAT ARE YOU GOING TO CHOOSE?

||| Get ready |||

1. In your opinion, what do the images represent?

   _____

   _____

2. Have you ever had to make a difficult choice in your life? What was it? How did you decide? Why?

   _____

   _____

3. Thinking about your routine. What is the most important thing you are going to do this week?

   _____

Let's practice

1 Read the following article on decision-making.

What to do – making decisions

What is decision making?

We make heaps of decisions or choices every day. Some of them are pretty easy, like what you wear to school – especially when you know you have to wear a school uniform anyway!

Some may be harder – like who you will play with, choosing after school activities or who you'll invite to your birthday party.

Others may be really hard, like should you just stand and watch someone being bullied? Should you take part in something which could lead to you or your friends getting into trouble?

As you grow up the number of choices you are faced with every day grows too.

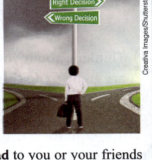

Making the right choices

When you are young, adults make most of the decisions for you, but there are still times when you have to decide things for yourself.

Making decisions can lead to consequences which can be good or bad.

Here are some tips which may help you. Writing down these steps and working through them can be really helpful if it is a big problem.

• **Define** the problem. **Work out** what it is you have to make a decision about.
• **Brainstorm** all the possible solutions.
• **Evaluate** all your ideas and consider what would be the consequences of each.
• **Decide** on a solution and carry it out. [...]

Accept responsibility for your decisions

Once you have made a decision, particularly an important decision, then you must be prepared to accept the consequences. Some may be more serious than others. [...]

Available at: <www.cyh.com/HealthTopics/HealthTopicDetails Kids.aspx?p=335&np=287&id=2975>. Access: Aug. 2018.

GLOSSARY

Carry it out (to carry out): execute, ponha em prática (executar, pôr em prática).

Decision making: tomada de decisão.

Faced with (to face with): defrontado com (defrontar-se com).

Heaps: grande quantidade.

Lead (to lead): levar a.

Stand (to stand): parar.

Tips: dicas.

Trouble: problema.

Work out (to work out): defina (definir).

a) Now, mark **T** (true) or **F** (false) according to what you've read.

- ( ) It can be very hard to choose what to wear.
- ( ) Things like choosing people for your birthday party and who you are going to play with are quite simple.
- ( ) As you grow older, you will have more decisions to make.
- ( ) Young people can make most decisions by themselves.
- ( ) Your wrong decisions can bring you bad consequences.
- ( ) Writing down the problems can make them worse.
- ( ) Once you evaluate the problem, you have to decide what to do and follow through with it.

b) Read the definitions below and write which tip from the text is it.

- Think about all the possible courses of action. _____
- Choose the best solution and realize it. _____
- Find out what it is you need to decide upon. _____
- Think of pros and cons of every course of action. _____

(2) Now, in pairs, interview each other and take notes.

	Questions	My answer	My friend's answer
a)	Do you make choices by yourself, or do you need help with it? Why?		
b)	What is a bad decision? How do you deal with it?		
c)	Do you take responsibility for your choices?		
d)	How do you make a decision? Are you an indecisive person?		
e)	Is it easy for you to make choices?		
f)	Once you've decided something, do you stick with it or do you change it easily?		
g)	Is it correct to assume that, as soon as you make a decision, you have agreed upon a plan to do something?		

Let's listen n' speak

TRACK 04

1 **Listen to Jimmy and check all the options that applies.**

a) ◯ Jimmy gave Rodney a piggyback ride.

b) ◯ Jimmy is going to walk to school every day.

c) ◯ Jimmy takes a nap every day after school.

d) ◯ Jimmy is not going to take a nap after school.

e) ◯ Jimmy's father is going to ban the afternoon naps.

f) ◯ Rodney sleeps less than Jimmy.

g) ◯ Rodney gave Jimmy a piggyback ride.

h) ◯ The school is going to offer bus rides.

stockfour/Shutterstock.com

2 **Listen to Jimmy again and answer.**

a) Who is Rodney?

_____

b) Why did he need to take a piggyback ride with him?

_____

c) What does Jimmy think the school should provide?

_____

d) What is Jimmy's expertise now?

_____

e) Is his father happy with his afternoon routine?

_____

3 **Pair up and discuss the following topics.**

- How do you go to school? How long does it take?
- What do you usually do after school? What are your free-time activities?
- Is there anything that you do and your parents don't appreciate? What is it?

CHAPTER 2

Let's practice

1 Read the comic strip and answer the questions.

a) What is the comic strip about?

_____

b) What does Lucy want from Charlie Brown? Why?

_____

c) How does Charlie Brown react to the plan Lucy shows him?

_____

d) What does Lucy do? Why?

_____

e) What happens to Charlie Brown?

_____

2 **Look at the following sentence.**

> This year I'm gonna [*going to*] kick that ball clear out of the universe!

a) Choose the best option:

- ( ) Charlie Brown has already kicked the ball.
- ( ) Charlie Brown has decided to kick the ball.

b) Which tense idea do we get from the verb in the setence?

- ( ) Present.
- ( ) Past.
- ( ) Future.

3 **Circle the correct option.**

a) Look. Dark clouds in the sky. It (is going to / going to) rain.

b) Atchim!! Oh, I (am going/ am going to) get a cold.

c) There is a traffic jam, so we (going to/ are going to) be very late.

d) Why did Lana put all these things on the kitchen table? She (is going to/is go to) make pancakes.

4 **Write affirmative sentences in the future using the given prompts.**

a) I/order/a cake _____

b) My mom/pick up/the sweets _____

c) My dad/set the table _____

d) My brother/decorate/the house _____

e) My sister/prepare a playlist _____

5 **It is Henry's test week at school. He needs to study, so he cannot do these things. Write negative sentences.**

a) go out _____

b) watch TV _____

c) use the iPad _____

d) sleep at his friend's _____

e) ride his bicycle _____

> **LANGUAGE PIECE**
>
> **Future: be going to Affirmative**
>
> **Subject pronoun** + **be (is/ am/are)** + **going to** + **verb (infinitive)** + **complement**.
>
> **They are going to be mathematicians.**

26

6 Rewrite the following sentences in the negative form of the future with **goint to.**

a) I am going to the Philippines next week.

_____

b) Our parents are going to ground us if we fail the finals.

_____

c) Jason is going to join the Olympic Swimming Team.

_____

d) We are going to the movies later today.

_____

e) Livia is going to buy a new dress for the party.

_____

7 Match the columns.

a) What are you going to do after class?

b) Who is going to help you with the homework?

c) When are they going to deliver the table ?

d) How are you going to go home with this rain?

e) Why is your dad going to have a surgery?

- ( ) On Thursday.
- ( ) Because his heart is not OK.
- ( ) By taxi.
- ( ) My older brother.
- ( ) Play video games.

8 Write questions with the given prompts.

a) to pick up at the airport

_____

b) to watch at the movies

_____

c) to visit Sue at the hospital

_____

> **LANGUAGE PIECE**
>
> **Future: be going to**
> **Negative**
>
> **Subject pronoun + be (is/am/ are) + not + going to + verb (infinitive) + complement.**
>
> **I am not going to travel to Hawaii.**
> **Interrogative**
> **Be (is/am/are) + subject pronoun + going to + verb (infinitive) + complement.**
>
> **Is Liam going to arrive before 6 p.m.?**

TRACK 05

> **Vocabulary hint**
> **Going to contraction**
>
> In spoken English it is common the contraction of the expression *going to* become *gonna*. Pay attention:
>
> **I'm gonna** go shopping tomorrow.
>
> She**'s gonna** come home with Sue.
>
> They**'re gonna** take a trip to California.

1 Check the correct option to complete the sentences.

a) Carol is _____ about later on.
- ◯ sad
- ◯ excited

b) Betty is going to organize her books _____.
- ◯ next week
- ◯ in a short while

c) Betty is going to study for _____.
- ◯ an exam
- ◯ a piano recital

d) Betty wants to _____ the phone call.
- ◯ continue
- ◯ finish

e) Carol _____ Gael.
- ◯ does not know
- ◯ knows

f) Carol _____ herself to go out with them.
- ◯ invites
- ◯ knows

2 Who said that? Use **B** for Betty and **C** for Carol.

a) ◯ Sorry, I'm very busy.
b) ◯ The test is in three weeks.
c) ◯ What's wrong?
d) ◯ We're kind of dating.
e) ◯ I know you hate him.

3 Circle the incorrect information and rewrite the sentences correcting them.

a) Betty is going to organize her city maquette.

b) Betty is going to finish her book.

c) Carol considers Gael a great guy.

d) Carol asks if she can offer them a ride.

4 Pair up and chat about your plans for: tonight, tomorrow and next weekend.

28

Let's read n' write

1 Do you know what you are going to do in the future? Read Maria's essay and answer the questions.

August 10, 2018.

My Future

Some of my friends have no idea where they want to go from high school. I, **on the other hand**, have most of my future already **planned out based off** of goals, hopes, and dreams. Knowing what I want in my life relieves a lot of stress and worry. I have no idea where I'm going to go, but at least I know how I want to get there. I know my college goals, how I want my lifestyle to be, and what I want to do with my free time.

First off, my main goal is to go to a good college and get a degree that won't make me **bang** my head against a wall with frustration. Another thing about my future life is I'm in **high hopes** I'll have a good job. That is going to get me a decent home, money to spend on traveling, and other things I want to do to feel happy.

Last thing about my future is what I'm going to do in my spare time. One hobby I have is writing. Writing for me is like documenting all the important times in my life worth remembering and how I feel about them. I really want to travel a lot when I get older too. One last thing, I'd like to have an exciting social life, and fun people to share good times with.

I think, no matter what happens to me, my future is going to be very exciting and I'll never have to follow a boring routine. So that's what I want my life to be like. **Wrapping up**, I want to reach my goals in college, live my dream lifestyle, and **keep up** with the hobbies and **pastimes** I have always loved. A spontaneous, yet **laid back** life is perfect for me.

Maria T., Albany, New York.

GLOSSARY

Bang (to bang): bater.

Based off (to base off): baseado (basear).

High hopes: grandes esperanças.

Keep up: acompanhar, manter.

Laid back: descontraído.

On the other hand: por outro lado.

Pastimes: passatempos.

Planned out (to plan out): planejado (planejar).

Wrapping up (to wrap up): resumindo, concluindo (resumir, concluir).

a) Mark **T** (true) or **F** (false) according to Maria's future plans.

- ( ) Maria is stressed and worried about her future.
- ( ) Maria knows exactly where she is going to go.
- ( ) Maria has decided what her college and lifestyle goals are.
- ( ) Maria is worried that her college degree is going to make her unhappy.
- ( ) Maria is very positive about her job expectation.
- ( ) Maria is planning on expending her free time with her favorite hobbies.
- ( ) Maria is not expecting to travel a lot.
- ( ) Maria is sure her future is going to be very exciting.

b) What life aspects does Maria talk about in her essay?

- ( ) Career expectations.
- ( ) College degree.
- ( ) Exercise.
- ( ) Hobbies and travel.
- ( ) Personal life.
- ( ) Retirement plans.

(2) Read the text again and think about its aspects.

a) What kind of text is it?

_____

b) How is it organized?

_____

c) How many parts does the essay present?

_____

_____

d) What kind of text is an essay?

- ( ) Descriptive.
- ( ) Narrative.
- ( ) Persuasive.

e) What kind of language was used in the essay? Give examples.

_____

_____

3 Now, use your knowledge about essays and write one about your future plans. Take a look at the tips below.

Steps
- Think about specific details and expectations regarding studies, career, personal life, hobbies, lifestyle etc.
- Organize the structure: introduction, development, closing.
- Draft the outline.

||| Citizenship moment |||

Citizenship

Elections 101

Why voting matters

The government — whether it's in Washington, DC, in your state, or in your **hometown** — affects your life, and by voting you get to say what's important to you, and you say it straight to the politicians.

It makes us equal

Each of us (when we're old enough) has one and only one vote. Voting is one of the few times when all **grown-ups** in the U.S. have an equal say. No matter how much money you have or who your friends are, you only get one vote.

Each vote sends a message

Even if the person you vote for loses, your vote matters because it lets winners and losers know who supports their points of view.

Whoever wins has the power to impact your life

The government is in charge of making important decisions that impact almost every aspect of your life, like:

- Your school, such as what gets taught, how many kids are in your class.
- The environment, including how clean your air and water will be, how we'll deal with global warming problems.
- Your health, including whether or not you and your family can get **health insurance**, how much it costs to go to the doctor or to buy **prescription drugs**.
- Who gets to visit, work and live in our country. If some members of your family live in another country and would like to move here, the federal government controls whether or not they can.
- Your safety, including how big your police and fire departments are.
- How much money we spend on the military and whether we go to war. What happens now has a great effect on the future.

||| GLOSSARY

Grown-ups: adultos.

Health insurance: seguro-saúde.

Hometown: cidade natal.

Prescription drugs: remédios prescritos com receita médica.

Citizenship

If you think that your opinion doesn't matter about who's president now, think again! The people in office now are making decisions that will affect your life now AND later! This is why it's important to get involved and be heard now, even when you can't vote.

Based on: PBS Kids. Available at: <http://pbskids.org/zoom/fromyou/elections/elections101.html>. Access: Aug. 2018.

Let's practice

1) What type of political system does your country have?

_____

_____

2) Discuss with your classmates and take notes on your notebook.

a) Who are the mayor of your city, the governor of your state, and the president of Brazil?

b) Do you think too much money is spent on campaigns?

c) What is your opinion about celebrities who run for a position in politics?

d) Who is the most controversial politician in your country? Why?

e) Why is voting an important responsibility of a citizen?

f) When will you be able to vote for the first time?

g) How will you choose your candidates?

h) Should voting be compulsory?

PROJECT

Political systems

Organize yourself into five groups and choose one of the following political systems to research about:

- Democracy.
- Republic.
- Monarchy.
- Communism.
- Dictatorship.

Once you gather all the information, make a chart and present to your classmates.

REVIEW

1 Sebastian has many plans for his future. There are six of them hidden at the word search below. Can you find them?

A	S	D	F	G	H	J	K	L	Q	W	E	R	T	G
Y	U	I	O	P	A	S	D	F	G	H	J	K	L	E
G	O	A	B	R	O	A	D	C	V	B	N	B	M	T
Z	X	C	V	B	N	M	A	E	I	O	U	U	B	A
C	D	F	G	H	J	K	L	M	N	P	Q	Y	R	J
S	T	V	S	S	T	V	S	S	T	V	R	A	Q	O
S	T	V	X	W	Z	A	B	C	D	E	F	H	G	B
H	I	J	K	L	M	N	O	P	Q	R	S	O	T	T
G	U	V	S	T	V	S	T	V	E	I	O	U	U	S
R	C	D	E	F	G	H	I	J	K	L	M	S	N	P
A	P	P	L	Y	F	O	R	C	O	L	L	E	G	E
D	K	L	M	N	O	P	Q	R	K	L	M	N	O	P
U	U	V	X	Z	S	T	V	S	E	I	U	V	X	Z
A	G	H	G	E	T	M	A	R	R	I	E	D	G	F
T	V	X	Z	K	W	Y	A	E	I	V	X	Z	K	W
E	D	E	F	G	H	I	J	K	L	D	E	F	G	H

Sebastian plans are...

a) _____

c) _____

e) _____

b) _____

d) _____

f) _____

2 Write questions for the following answers.

a) _____

Yes, I am definitely going to be late.

b) _____

Yes, he is going to visit his friend at the hospital.

c) _____

No, we won't live in this country when we get married. We dream of living in Australia.

d) _____

No, I am not going to the movies with Bob. I'm going to a concert with him.

3 **Transform the sentences in their opposite: the affirmatives into negatives and vice-versa.**

a) Ines will buy a motorhome.

_____

b) They won't retire.

_____

c) Gilson will not get a new skate.

_____

d) The Gastons will have another baby.

_____

e) Neide won't get a PhD in Math.

_____

4 **Match the questions and the answers:**

a) What do you hope to do in your life? • ( ) Yes, I would love to live on Saturn!

b) Where do you plan on going in the future? • ( ) I hope to graduate and find a good job.

c) Would you want to live on another planet? • ( ) I think we won't have books at schools.

d) What will education be like in the future? • ( ) I plan on going to Europe in the future.

e) What are you going to do when you finish school? • ( ) In that case, I am going to move to another city.

5 **Complete the sentences using if, so, because or then.**

a) Steve is not going to the rock concert _____ he doesn't like rock.

b) I have the tickets, _____ I am going to the movies.

c) I will travel with you _____ my parents allow me.

d) First they will do their homework, and _____ they will play.

DO NOT FORGET!

Future .... **Will** or **to be going to**

Will

Use **will** to talk about the future in general, for ideas and wishes not involving concrete decisions and for decisions made at the time speaking,

AFFIRMATIVE: Subject + will + verb (infinitive) + complement.

EXAMPLES: I think she will arrive around 7 p.m.

He thinks he'll have a new car in a year time.

NEGATIVE: Subject + will + NOT + verb (infinitive) + complement.

EXAMPLES: I think she will not arrive around 7 p.m.

He thinks he won't have a new car in a year time.

INTERROGATIVE: Will + subject + verb (infinitive) + complement?

EXAMPLES: Will she arrive around 7 p.m.?

Will he have a new car in a year time?

To be going to

Use **to be going to** to talk about concrete plans and decisions about the future, and when there is evidence something is going to happen, a certain result will come from the moment conditions.

AFFIRMATIVE: Subject + verb to be + going to + verb (infinitive) + complement.

EXAMPLES: I am going to travel this evening.

He is going to school tomorrow.

NEGATIVE: Subject + verb to be + NOT + going to + verb (infinitive) + complement.

EXAMPLES: I am not going to travel this evening.

He is not going to school tomorrow.

INTERROGATIVE: Verb to be + subject + going to + verb (infinitive) + complement?

EXAMPLES: Am I going to travel this evening?

Is he going to school tomorrow?

CONJUNCTIONS
Words that connect clauses or phrases.

SO — shows the result or consequence of a fact.

BECAUSE — explains the reason for something to happen.

IF — expresses a condition for something to happen.

THEN — explains the sequence in which things happen.

EXAMPLES

I'm your mother, **so** I can tell you what to do, and I'm telling you not to go to that concert!

I can't go to the concert **because** my mother doesn't allow me.

Mike will only go to the concert **if** his mother allows him.

Mike will wash the dishes and **then** he will ask again his mom's permission to go to the concert.

36

OVERCOMING CHALLENGES

(FUVEST – 2011)

Europe's economic distress could be China's opportunity. In the past, the country has proved a hesitant investor in the continent, but figures show a 30 percent surge in new Chinese projects in Europe last year. And these days Europe looks ever more tempting. Bargains proliferate as the yuan strengthens and cash-strapped governments forget concerns over foreign ownership of key assets. On a recent visit to Greece, Vice Premier Zhang Dejiang sealed 14 deals, reportedly the largest Chinese investment package in Europe, covering a range of sectors from construction to telecoms.

Meanwhile, Irish authorities have opened talks with Chinese promoters to develop a 240-hectare industrial park in central Ireland where Chinese manufacturers could operate inside the European Union free of quotas and costly tariffs. In time, that could bring 10,000 new jobs. "It's good business," says Vanessa Rossi, an authority on China at the Royal Institute of International Affairs in London. "There's big mutual benefit here." Europe needs money; China needs markets.

Newsweek, July 19, 2010, p. 6. Adaptado.

1 **Segundo o texto, a China**

a) aproveitou o momento da crise mundial e fez vários investimentos no próprio país.

b) teve problemas econômicos similares aos dos países europeus, mas conseguiu superá-los.

c) hesitava em investir em países asiáticos e perdeu boas oportunidades na região.

d) aumentou seus investimentos na Europa no ano passado.

e) ressurgiu como potência mundial após vários anos de isolamento.

2 **Afirma-se, no texto, que a Irlanda**

a) negocia com a China o desenvolvimento de um parque industrial que trará benefícios à Europa e à própria China.

b) possui um plano de desenvolvimento que exime os investidores de pagamento de impostos.

c) enfrenta sérios problemas de desemprego, que já afetaram dez mil trabalhadores.

d) deseja fechar acordos que envolvam outros países da União Europeia.

e) planeja as mudanças que pretende implementar junto à Câmara Real de Negócios Internacionais, em Londres.

UNIT 3
HOW ARE THEY GOING TO TRAVEL?

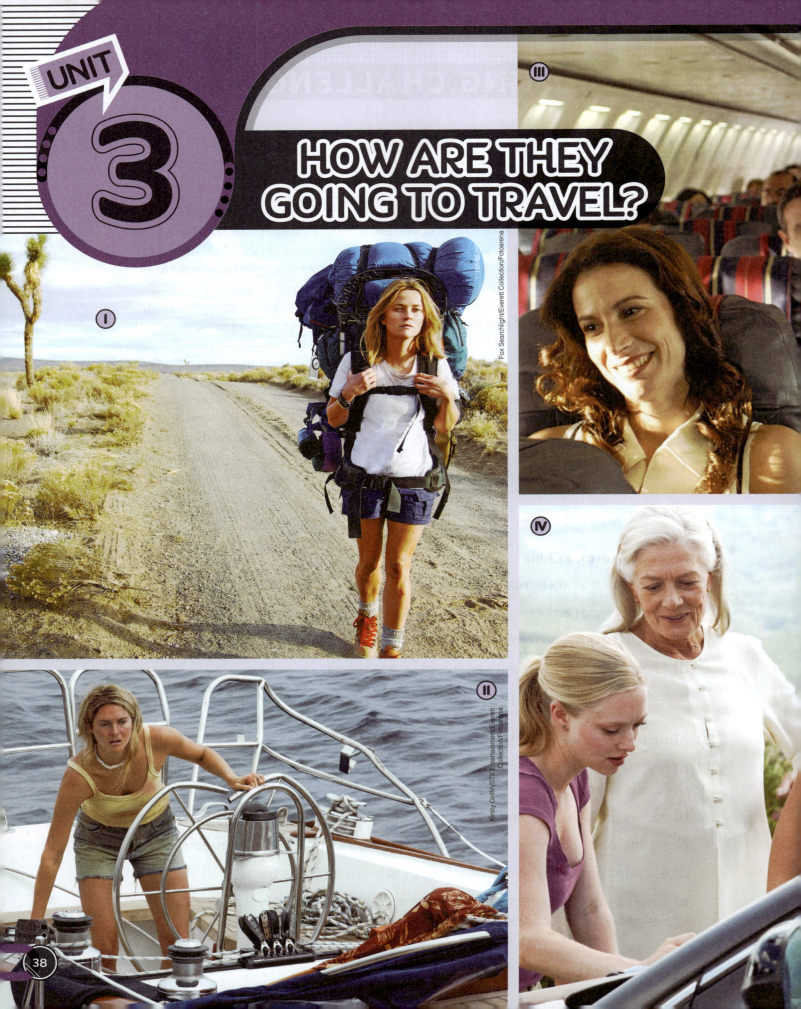

||| Get ready |||

1 What kind of activity is shown in the pictures?

_____

2 What means of transportation are shown in the pictures? Match the options with the pictures.

- ◯ Bus.
- ◯ Train.
- ◯ Airplane.
- ◯ Car.

- ◯ Motorcycle.
- ◯ Foot.
- ◯ Boat.
- ◯ Truck.

3 Discuss with a partner.

a) Which means of transportation have you already used?

b) Which means of transportation would you like to try?

c) Which means of transportation seems to be more dangerous? Why?

d) Which means of transportation seems to be safer? Why?

CHAPTER 1

Let's practice

1 Classify the means of transportations accordingly to where they are used.

> airplane • ambulance • bike • bus • canoe • car • ferry boat
> glider • helicopter • hot air balloon • motorbike • on foot • rocket
> sail boat • ship • speed boat • subway • train • truck

By land	By air	By water

2 Use the adjectives below to describe the following means of transportation.

> big • boring • cheap • comfortable • convenient
> enjoyable • expensive • fast • hasty • heavy • light
> rapid • slow • small • speeding • swift • tiring • wide

a) car _____

b) helicopter _____

c) speed boat _____

d) train _____

e) balloon _____

f) ferry boat _____

40

Let's listen n' speak

1 Listen to the reading of a travel article and complete it with the missing words.

Life Style

What are the different ways of travelling?

There are a handful ways of traveling across the globe. People can travel as much by water, as by _____, or air. These ways of traveling may be used alone, or a _____ may be needed depending on the traveler's desires and needs, or other arrangements may be necessary, such as **accommodations** for **overnight** stays in certain _____.

One of the most **recognized** ways of travelling by water is the cruise travel, however the cruises not necessarily circle the globe, actually, most of them travel throughout a specific geographical region. When it comes to land, _____, _____, and _____ are the main ways used to move around. Train accommodations are usually more comfortable than on _____, as some trains **allow** passengers to **book** private rooms. Cars, on the other hand, despite being a much more private way of travelling, are also **tiring**, once they don't have the convenience of the other means of transportation.

Other option when travelling is through the _____ on _____ and many airlines offer **ticket** promotion once it is a costly way of travelling.

When not **aboard** a _____, _____, or _____, travelers may need a place to stay overnight. Hotels and **hostels** are the more common options, but they can get _____.

Based on: wiseGEEK. Available at: <www.wisegeek.com/what-are-the-different-ways-to-travel-the-world.htm>. Access: May 2018.

GLOSSARY

Aboard: a bordo.
Accommodations: acomodações.
Allow (to allow): permitir.
Book (to book): reservar.
Hostels: albergues.
Overnight: durante a noite.
Recognized (to recognize): reconhecidos.
Ticket: bilhete, passagem.
Tiring: cansativo.

2 **Listen to the audio again and answer the questions:**

a) According to the text, what are the different ways to travel?

_____

b) "Cruise travel is one of the most recognized ways to travel the world." Do you know what a cruise is? Which way does it travel, by air, land, or water?

_____

c) According to the text, which way is more comfortable: bus or train? Why?

_____

3 **What is it? Read the definition and choose the word they refer to.**

suitcase • postcard • passport • border • duty-free • currency

a) A thing to carry clothes and belongings when you travel. _____

b) A document necessary to enter foreign countries. _____

c) A card with a message. _____

d) An imaginary line separating one country or state from another. _____

e) The money that a country uses. _____

f) Not taxed when taken into another country. _____

4 **Choose the best option to complete the sentences.**

a) The (flight / fly) from Buenos Aires to New Zealand took 17 hours! I've never stayed so long on a plane before!

b) I like to (travel / trip) alone because I have to talk a lot and it helps to improve my English.

c) Last summer I went to Paris. It was the best (travel / trip) of my life.

d) If you want to go to New Orleans on Mardi Gras, you have to make a hotel (reserve / reservation) months before.

e) When in New York, you should see a Broadway show, you'll love it. It is guaranteed (satisfy / satisfaction)!

f) My friend Roberto invited me to Florence, so that he can (introduce / introduction) me to real Italian food.

5 **Do you have a dream trip? Write about it on your notebook and, then, share it with your classmates.**

Let's practice

1) Match the direct questions to their embedded versions.

a) How long does the bus ride to Niagara Falls take?

b) Where is the hostel?

c) When is the next movie session?

- ( ) Do you know when the next movie session is?
- ( ) Can you tell where the hostel is?
- ( ) Would you tell me how long the bus ride to Niagara Falls takes?

2) Write direct questions to the following answers.

a) _____

The nearest bus station is on Main Street.

b) _____

The mall opens at 10 a.m. on Sundays.

c) _____

A ticket for the CN Tower costs C$ 38.00.

3) Now, rewrite the questions from the previous activity in their embedded form.

a) _____
_____

b) _____
_____

c) _____
_____

LANGUAGE PIECE

Embedded question is a question that appears to be a declarative statement or a question in another question.

Can you tell me where you work?

Direct question is the "normal" question we ask people.

Where do you work?

4) Choose the correct embedded questions.

a) ( ) Could you tell me what your favorite subject is?

b) ( ) Could you tell me what is your favorite subject?

c) ( ) Can you tell me how long you have been studying at this school?

d) ( ) Can you tell me how long have you been studying at this school?

Let's listen n' speak

1 Listen to Ana and David and answer the following questions.

a) Why isn't the woman going to the park?
_____

b) What does the man think will happen over the weekend?
_____

c) What is the woman going to do on the weekend?
_____

d) Who is going to help with the cooking?
_____

e) What does the man offer to bring for the party?
_____

f) What is going to be special about the pool party?
_____

2 On your notebook, use the information below to write sentences about the people in the conversation.

Ana	David
Go to the park Have a pool party Hire a DJ	Go to the park Cook some pasta Bring a cake

3 Party planning. Imagine you and your friend are planning a party for the weekend. Discuss the questions below and write down your plans.

- When is the party going to be?
- Where is it going to happen?
- What is the theme of the party going to be?
- Who are you going to invite?
- What foods are you going to prepare?
- Is there going to be a special attraction?

Let's practice

1) Complete the sentences with will or be going to.

a) "There's no milk."
"I know, I _____ get some from the shop."

b) "We don't have any bread."
"Really? I _____ go to the grocery store right now."

c) "Why do you need to borrow my suitcase?"
"I _____ visit my sister in Canada next July."

d) "Oh, your phone is ringing!"
"I _____ get it!"

e) "Excuse Miss, are you ready to order?"
"I _____ have the burger and fries, please."

2) Match the columns.

a) What time is the train going to leave?   • ( ) Jane is going to go to the mall.

b) What will you have?   • ( ) I'm sure it's going to rain. I feel it in my bones.

c) What is she going to do tonight?   • ( ) I don't know. I'll look up this word in the dictionary.

d) What will happen at Bruno Mars concert?   • ( ) It is going to leave at 8 p.m.

e) When is Dana's party?   • ( ) It is going to take place next Saturday.

f) What's the meaning of awkward?   • ( ) I guess we will move to Paris next year.

g) When will you move?   • ( ) He will probably sing some of his new songs.

h) I think it will rain.   • ( ) I'll have a large pizza, please.

LANGUAGE PIECE

Will + **verb** (**infinitive**)
I **will call** you.

Be (**am/is/are**) + **going to** + **verb** (**infinitive**).
I **am going to visit** Sarah.

Vocabulary hint
Linking sounds – Consonant To Vowel (CTV)
It is the most frequently recurring word linking pattern in English.
Wake up   that's it   turn off

45

3. In groups of three, play this board game. Remember to use the future tense correctly so you can move forward.

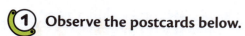 Let's read n' write

 Observe the postcards below.

I

II

GLOSSARY

Picnicking: fazer piquenique.
Rec'd (abbreviation of received – to receive): recebemos (receber).
Sightseeing: passeios.
Thrilled to death (idiom): very pleased and excited (expressão idiomática).

a) When were the postcards sent?

- I _____

- II _____

b) Where were they addressed to?

- I _____

- II _____

c) Who...

- is having fun sightseeing and picnicking? _____

- will be glad to see somebody again? _____

- has received postals? _____

- is thrilled to death? _____

(2) Analyze the text and answer.

a) Who are the postcards addressed to?

- ( ) Familiar people.
- ( ) Unknown people.

b) What kind of language is used in it?

- ( ) Informal.
- ( ) Formal.

c) What text elements support your previous answer? Give examples.

_____

d) What kind of information does it present?

- ( ) Dates.
- ( ) News.

- ( ) Geographic aspects.
- ( ) Personal experience.

- ( ) Specific locations.
- ( ) Travel tips.

e) What kind of text is it?

- ( ) Narrative.
- ( ) Short.
- ( ) Postcard.

- ( ) Descriptive.
- ( ) Essay.
- ( ) Long.

- ( ) Informative.
- ( ) Report.

f) Where can texts like this be found?

_____

48

g) What elements are part of this type of text?

- ( ) Address.
- ( ) Graphics and numbers.
- ( ) Handwriting.
- ( ) Sender.
- ( ) Subheadings.
- ( ) Date.

- ( ) Headline.
- ( ) Recipient.
- ( ) Stamp.
- ( ) Explanatory boxes.
- ( ) Postmark.
- ( ) Graphics and numbers.

(3) How about creating a postcard for a friend or relative? Follow the instructions.

- Choose someone to send the postcard to.
- Think about a topic to talk about in the postcard.
- Think of and look for all the information needed to complete the postcard.
- Write the text respecting the type of language usually used on postcards.
- Exchange compositions with a partner and correct it.
- Rewrite your postcard observing the corrections made.

CHAPTER 4
||| Tying in |||
THE EVOLUTION OF TRANSPORTATION

Walking
People have walked since ever. It has been a way to travel, and it is timeless.

6300 BC
People in the present-day Netherlands make dugout canoes from hollowed-out logs.

ANCIENT TIMES »»»

3000 BC
People create the covered wagon which aimed to transport goods and people from one place to another.

4000 BC
People in the Middle East start using animals to pull heavy loads.

4000 BC
People in Egypt discover how to join pieces of wood together, making larger long boats.

6000 BC
People in Scandinavia make wooden sleds to travel on snow.

Cristiane Viana

1769
Nicolas Joseph Cugnot designs the first self-propelled road vehicle with a steam engine.

1783
The Montgolfier Brothers invent the first hot-air balloon.

1787
The first successful trail of steamboat is made.

1816
The first bicycle is invented by German Baron Karl von Drais and was called Draisine.

PAVING THE WAY »»»

1865
People in Scotland lay the first concrete pavement.

1862
The first passenger ship starts to be used. Etienne Lenoir creates the first automobile with gasoline engine.

1833
Stockton and Darlington Railway create the first passenger train.

GLOSSARY

Ancient: antigo.
Dugout: abrigo.
Engine: motor.
Hollowed-out: oca, esvaziada.
Hybrid: híbrido.
Launches (to launch): lança (lançar).
Liquid-fueled: abastecido por líquido.
Loads: cargas.
Logs: registros.
Manned: tripulado.
Pavement: pavimento.
Rail line: linha de trem.
Releases (to release): lança (lançar).
Self-propeled: auto impulsionado.
Sleds: trenós.
Steam engine: motor a vapor.
Steamboat: barco a vapor.
Timeless: eterno, atemporal.
Wagon: carroça.

1903
The Wright Brothers invent and fly the first airplane.

1919
The first passenger plane flies across the English channel.

1926
Robert Goddard launches the first liquid-fueled rocket.

1940
Modern-day helicopters are designed.

NEW TIMES »»»

1969
Apollo is the first manned mission launched to the Moon.

1957
Sputnik I is the first man-made satellite to be launched into space.

1947
The first supersonic flight is launched.

2000
Toyota releases the first four-door, gas-electric hybrid car.

2002
Shanghai opens the first magnetic levitation rail line.

2004
The first manned private space flight is made by SpaceShipOne.

CONTEMPORARY ERA »»»

Based on: *History of Movement: the Evolution of Transportation*, available at: <www.tiki-toki.com/timeline/entry/279300/History-of-Movement-the-Evolution-of-Transportation/#vars!date=1752-10-20_03:59:02!>; *Ancient Egypt: Boats and Transportation*, available at: <www.ducksters.com/history/ancient_egypt/boats_and_transportation.php>. *Transportation Timeline*, available at: <https://wheelzine.com/transportation-timeline>. Access: Aug. 2018.

50

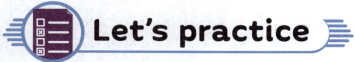

Let's practice

1 Answer according to the infographic.

a) When was the first steamboat made?
_____
_____

b) Who invented the first bicycle?
_____
_____

c) Who launched the first liquid-fueled rocket?
_____
_____

d) What is the timeless means of transportation?
_____
_____

e) What was the material used to make the first canoes?
_____
_____

f) Who created the first automobile gasoline engine?
_____
_____

g) What was the first manned mission launched to the Moon called?
_____
_____

h) Who made the first manned private space flight?
_____
_____

EXPLORING

SAHO – Transport on land
- www.sahistory.org.za/article/transport-land

e2 transport
- www.pbs.org/e2/transport.html

EXPLORING

- www.youtube.com/watch?v=5rg7vgniCZc
- www.youtube.com/watch?v=2-s4K3cBRxk

PROJECT

Brazil transportation technology

Team up, research about the different means of transportation and the technologies used in the Brazilian Transport System.

51

UNIT 4

SHOULD WE BE MORE CAREFUL?

||| Get ready |||

1) What are these movie scenes about?

_____

_____

2) Complete the table with your own answers and then interview a partner.

How many...	Your answers	Your partner's answers
...TV sets are there in your house?		
...cell phones are there?		
...computers are there?		
...digital cameras are there?		
...music devices are there?		

3) Discuss in small groups.

a) Are you familiar with different types of technology? Which ones?

b) What technological devices do you use?

c) Are these technologies available in Brazil? Does everybody have equal access to them?

d) In your opinion, how different were people's lives before the development of these technologies?

e) What are the consequences of constant use of technology?

f) What about social media? What are the pros and cons of it?

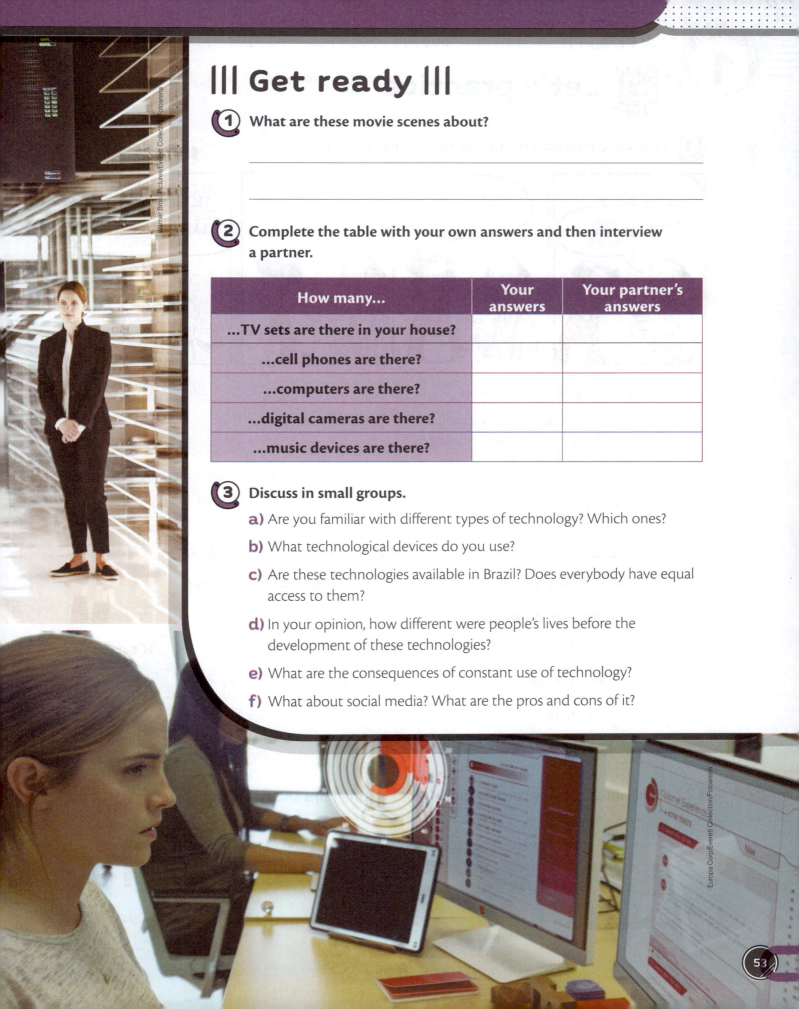

Let's practice

1 Read the comic strip below and answer the questions.

a) The comic strip above is about…

- ◯ … the difficulty of keeping up with the latest technology because it is always evolving.
- ◯ … the easiness of keeping up with the latest technology because it is always evolving.

GLOSSARY
Latest: mais recente.

b) Discuss with your classmates.
- Do you identify with the character? Why or why not?
- What do you think about the speed with which technology has been evolving?

c) Which technologies and programs do you use to communicate with others?

- ◯ Instant messaging.
- ◯ Social networking sites.
- ◯ Smartphone.
- ◯ Computer.
- ◯ Tablet.
- ◯ Laptop.
- ◯ Email.
- ◯ Texting.
- ◯ Tweeting.
- ◯ Blogs.
- ◯ Video chat.
- ◯ Chat room.
- ◯ Forum.
- ◯ VoIP.

2 Think about the way you use the devices and programs and talk with a partner.

- How often do you use messaging apps?
- Do you use abbreviations when chatting on the internet?
- Do you use emoticons?
- How many hours do you stay online on a daily basis?
- How many different media and devices do you use per day?

3 Let's talk about abbreviations. Match the abbreviations to their meanings.

a) LOL
b) BRB
c) AFK
d) OMG
e) IDK
f) IMO
g) ASAP
h) ROFL

- Laughing out loud.
- Away from the keyboard.
- I don't know.
- Be right back.
- Oh, my God.
- In my opinion.
- Rolling on the floor laughing.
- As soon as possible.

4 What do these emoticons express? Choose the best option.

a)
- ◯ Happy.
- ◯ Sad.

d)
- ◯ Excited.
- ◯ Bored.

g)
- ◯ Confused.
- ◯ Funny.

b)
- ◯ Funny.
- ◯ Bored.

e)
- ◯ Fear.
- ◯ Surprised.

h)
- ◯ Peaceful.
- ◯ Bored.

c)
- ◯ Confused.
- ◯ Embarrased.

f)
- ◯ Sleepy.
- ◯ In love.

i)
- ◯ Excited.
- ◯ Angry.

Ilustrações: João P. Mazzoco

5 What is your favorite emoticon? Why?

Let's listen n' speak

1 Kevin and Anabel are chatting. Listen to their conversation and complete the gaps.

antivirus • technician • went off • format • type up • backup • hacked into • email

Hi, Kevin. How are you?

Hi, Anabel, I'm just fine… but I've been having problems with my computer… Anyway, what about you?

I'm fine too... What kinds of problems?

Someone _____ it. I was surfing on the net when suddenly it _____.

OMG! What did you do?

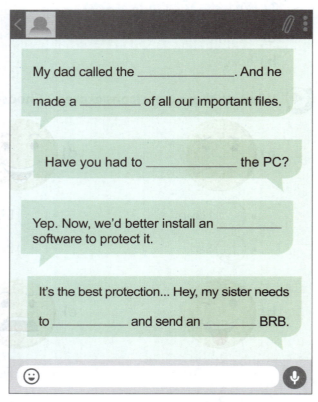

My dad called the _____. And he made a _____ of all our important files.

Have you had to _____ the PC?

Yep. Now, we'd better install an _____ software to protect it.

It's the best protection... Hey, my sister needs to _____ and send an _____ BRB.

2 Listen again to Kevin and Anabel's chat and answer the questions:

a) Why did Kevin's PC go off?

_____

b) What did the technician do before formatting the PC?

_____

c) What does Kevin need to do now?

_____

d) What about you? Have you ever had a situation like this? If so, what happened?

_____

CHAPTER 2

Let's practice

1 **Write sentences with should, had better and ought to. Use the cues in parentheses.**

a) It's late. You have classes tomorrow. (should / turn off / cell phone)

_____

_____

b) My presentation is tomorrow. (ought to / finish printing)

_____

_____

c) My parents are video calling me. (had better / turn on / the computer)

_____

d) My appointment is at 2 p.m. (had better / not / late)

_____

> **LANGUAGE PIECE**
>
> **Modal verbs**
>
> | | |
> |---|---|
> | **Should** | Less formal, it is used in advice and suggestions. |
> | **Had better** | More formal, used to give recommendations, for desperate comments, and warnings. |
> | **Ought to** | More formal, it is used in advices and suggestions. It doesn't have interrogative form. |

2 **Rewrite the sentences below correcting the mistakes.**

a) Danielle would better arrive soon, or she will miss the movie.

_____

b) Mark should wears a jacket, it is cold outside.

_____

c) I ought to asking for my parent's advice about the internet use.

_____

3 **Match the columns with the correct information about the modal verbs.**

a) should • ( ) It indicates a warning.

b) had better • ( ) It is more jornal.

c) ought to • ( ) It is the most informal.

4 **Unscramble the words to make correct sentences.**

a) have / we / media / be / on / to / social / careful / network

_____

b) sharing / you / info / on / must / the / avoid / personal / internet

_____

c) need / antivirus / I / to / an / install / computer / my / on

_____

5 **Complete these sentences with the correct form of the modals must, have to and need to. Follow the clues.**

a) At my new school we _____ turn off our smartphones. (+)

b) You _____ share images without permission. (−)

c) You _____ turn off the computers now, other students will use them. (−)

d) There is a lot of virus online. I _____ install a good antivirus on my computer. (+)

e) You _____ turn off your cell phone during the speech. (+)

f) Jane _____ buy another cell phone. Her mother got her old one fixed. (−)

g) Jake _____ obey his parents' rules on the use of internet. (+)

h) Susan and Margo _____ delete their social media profile. They _____ review the info they share and be more careful. (−/+)

LANGUAGE PIECE

Modal verbs

Must	It expresses strong personal obligations.
Mustn't	It expresses that something is prohibited.
Have to	It expresses responsibilities in daily life.
Don't have to	It expresses that something is not required.
Need to	It expresses the importance of doing something.
Don't need to	It expresses that something is not necessary.

TRACK 02

Vocabulary hint
Modal verbs

Mustn't

Have to

Need to

Ought to

Had better

58

6 Get together in groups of three or four and play the "What should I do?" game. Every time you land on a space, read its sentence and make another one using: **had better**, **ought to**, **have to**, **need to** or **must**.

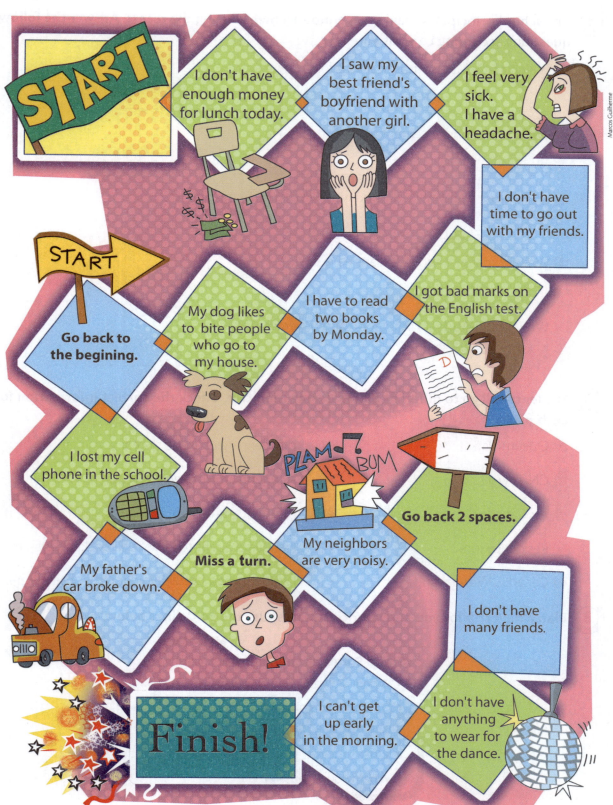

Let's listen n' speak

1) The school principal is making an announcement during the recess. Answer the following questions according to what you hear.

a) Which grade is the announcement for?
_____

b) What is the announcement about?
_____

c) What must be made until Sunday at 11 p.m.? How much is it?
_____

d) What do parents and guardians have to do?
_____

e) Why should students bring food and beverages for the ride?
_____

2) Students will go to different places during their trip. Check the correct information for each place:

a) Queen's Park • ( ) Students need to be rested.

b) CN Tower • ( ) Students don't need to go up.

c) Air Canada Centre • ( ) Students must have dinner.

d) Residence Inn • ( ) Students ought to leave their backpacks on the bus.

e) Canada's Wonderland • ( ) Students had better avoid internet use till late.

3) Plan a field trip for you and your classmates. Use the guidelines below.

Grade 9 end of the year field trip!
- Where are you going to go?
- How are you going to go?
- What do you need to bring?
- What shouldn't you forget?
- What should you do there?

Let's read n' write

1 Look at the symbols below and discuss the following questions with your classmates.

a) What are these symbols?

b) Which ones do you use?

c) Which ones help you contact friends?

d) Are you an active social network user?

e) How many social media accounts do you have?

f) Which social network is your favorite?

g) How often do you check your social media accounts?

2 Observe the following media profile and answer the questions.

A | 🔍 | Amelia | Homepage

Amelia
Edit Profile

≡ Activity Log

Timeline ▾ | About | Friends | Photos | Archive | More ▾

🌐 **Intro** Edit + Add info About You

Overview	
Work and Education	100%
Places She's Lived	100%
Contact and Basic Info	100%
Family and Relationships	100%
Details About Amelia	100%
Life Events	100%

Name
Amelia O'Donell

Birthday
02 April 2000

Hometown
Goiânia

Relationship Status
Single

Email
a_melia_o_donell@email.com

Telephone
(+55) 62 9 9596 1022

Family members See All

Suggested Friends All Friends 789 Recently Added Work Current City Hometown Search Friends 🔍

a) What kind of information can be seen on Amelia's profile?

_____

b) Does she have a big social network? What piece of information proves that?

_____

c) Does Amelia share many pictures on her social network? What piece of information proves that?

_____

d) What language is used in the network website? _____

e) What is the target public of this network? _____

f) How does Amelia interact on this social network?

_____

g) Do you think Amelia is an active network user? Why? Discuss with your classmates.

3 **What about you? Are you a social media addict? Take the quiz and find out.**

1.	I check my social network on my phone first thing in the morning.
2.	I take pictures of my meals and post them instantly.
3.	I ask my friends to check and to like my photos on social media.
4.	I check my social media accounts several times a day.
5.	I take a break and stay away from social media.
6.	I post things on my social media status several times a day.
7.	I know the number of my friends and followers on social media.
8.	I feel disappointed when my posts do not get many likes.
9.	I spend more than 3 hours a day on social media.
10.	I feel happy when I get lots of friend requests on social media.
	Total score

Never 0 pts	**Often 10 pts**	**0-10 Not an addict**	**51-100 Obsessed**
Occasionally 5 pts	**Always 20 pts**	**11-50 Moderate**	**101-200 Addicted**

4 **Think about the social network and discuss the following questions with your classmates.**

a) How do you stay connected with your friends nowadays?

b) Who are, in your opinion, the majority of social media users in the world?

c) What are the advantages and disadvantages of a social network?

d) Do all social media sites have the same status among internet users?

e) Do you consider to be safe to share your personal information on the social networks? Why or why not?

5 **Analyze the text and answer.**

a) What is the main characteristic of this kind of text?

- ( ) Descriptive.
- ( ) Narrative.
- ( ) Informative.

b) What kind of information does it present?

- ( ) Personal information.
- ( ) Cultural traditions.
- ( ) Historical facts.

c) What kind of language is used in it?

- ( ) Informal.
- ( ) Formal.

d) What elements are part of this type of text?

_____

_____

_____

_____

6 **Have you ever thought of creating a social network? Follow the instructions below and work in groups to get it done.**

a) Decide on the target public and the main language used.

b) Is it going to be a local or a global network?

c) What fields will it present? What is the goal in using each of them?

d) How will the members interact with it?

e) Is it going to be linked to other social networks?

f) How is it going to deal with privacy and safety of its members?

Discuss your ideas and share thoughts with your classmates. Follow your teacher's instructions to develop this project.

CHAPTER 4

||| Citizenship moment |||

THINGS TO COME
FUTURE TECHNOLOGY TIMELINE

Forecasting the future of technology is a shaky sort of structure. Take a look now on some of the best predictions about the future of technology made by futurists.

ZERO-SIZE INTELLIGENCE
Zero-sized chip casings and atom-powered transistors invisible to the naked eye.

MOVEMENT-CONTROLLED TECHNOLOGY
Machines that are controlled by gestures or eye movements base on face and movement recognition software.

CHEAP SOLAR POWER
Solar power widely available due to manufactured perovskite and organic solar cells near 100% efficiency.

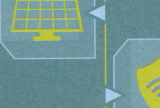

UNHACKABLE INTERNET
A fully secure internet created by a satellite network using entangled photons for quantum-key distribution (QKD).

NEUROHACKING
Machines capable of reading people's minds by decoding brainwaves.

FULLY IMMERSIVE COMPUTER INTERFACE
Advances in VR/AR, projection mapping, haptics, and brain-computer interface creates an intuitive interaction interface with entertainment, infotainment, and web-surfing.

MASS DATA
All the data, machine, and algorithms used to make sense of all the virtual space activity used to optimize the internet use.

NANOTECHNOLOGY, NANOMED
Used in every field for innovations, the nanotechnology allows with unbelievable precision to copy the work of nature at its most basic functioning level.

GLOSSARY

Casings: revestimentos, invólucros.
Decoding (to decode): decodificando (decodificar).
Entangled: emaranhado.
Forecasting (to forecast): prever.
Haptics: táteis.
Infotainment: entretenimento informativo.
Manufactured: fabricado.
Neurohacking: hackear o cérebro.
Perovskite: perovskita (mineral relativamente raro).
Photons: fótons (partículas que compõem a luz e transportam as energias contidas na radiação eletromagnética).
Predictions: previsões.
Shaky: instável.
Unhackable: que não pode ser hackeado.
Widely: amplamente.

Source: Infographic: A Timeline of Future Technology, available at: <www.visualcapitalist.com/timeline-future-technology/>; Future technology: 22 ideas about to change our world, available at: <www.sciencefocus.com/feature/future/future-technology-22-ideas-about-change-our-world>; 10 futurist Predictions in the World of Technology, available at: <https://electronics.howstuffworks.com/future-tech/10-futurist-predictions-in-the-world-of-technology.htm>. Access: Aug. 2018.

Let's practice

1 **What kinds of future technology are presented in the infographic?**

- ( ) Health care.
- ( ) Technology control.
- ( ) Clothing.
- ( ) Batteries.
- ( ) Space devices.
- ( ) Power sources.
- ( ) Internet safety.
- ( ) New materials.
- ( ) Internet interactions.
- ( ) Technology systems.

2 **What technology is it according to the text?**

a) It can copy things at their most basic function level.
_____

b) It is almost invisible to the naked eye.
_____

c) It has a brain-computer intuitive interaction.
_____

d) It is operated by movement recognition software.
_____

e) It is able to decode brainwaves.
_____

f) Technology used to understand the virtual space activity.
_____

g) It is widely available and organic.
_____

h) It is a fully secure satellite network.
_____

> **PROJECT**
>
> **Technological device timeline**
> Choose a modern gadget and research about it. Then, draw a timeline about its evolution and try to imagine how it can be improved in the future years.

> **▶❚❚ EXPLORING**
>
> - *Ready Players One*, 2018.
> - *Pacific Rim: Uprising*, 2018.
> - *Black Panther*, 2018.
> - *A Wrinkle in Time*, 2018.
> - *Replicas*, 2018.
> - *Ralph Breaks the Internet*, 2018.

3 **Discuss with your colleagues how these future technologies can help mankind.**

4 **Thinking about technology and how it interferes in the human communication, discuss the advantages and disadvantages of face-to-face and technological communication.**

REVIEW

1) All the embedded questions below have one mistake. Rewrite them in order to make them correct.

a) Do you know who is Michelle Obama?

b) Can you tell me how old are you?

c) Do you know where does Carlos live?

d) Can you to tell me when the next bus leaves?

2) Choose the best alternative to complete the sentences.

a) Stop, there is another car coming! We _____ crash!
- ( ) am going to
- ( ) are going to
- ( ) will

b) There is a good festival in town this summer. I _____ watch it.
- ( ) are going to
- ( ) will
- ( ) am going to

c) Maybe in the future everybody _____ stop using plastic items.
- ( ) will
- ( ) is going to
- ( ) are going to

d) Do you think it _____ be cold tomorrow morning?
- ( ) will
- ( ) is going to
- ( ) are going to

3) Rewrite the following text messages in standard English.

a) Talk 2 u later. _____

b) Imo, he's gr8! _____

c) Omg, I have to go now! Brb. _____

d) Call me asap! _____

4 **Choose the best option to correctly complete the sentences:**

a) _____ pay for the hotel room in advance?

- ◯ Do we must
- ◯ Do we to must
- ◯ Must we

b) Children _____ learn to read and write when they are in grade 1.

- ◯ must
- ◯ musts
- ◯ must to

c) We have _____ early because the play starts at 6 p.m.

- ◯ to leave
- ◯ leave
- ◯ leaves

d) I _____ get up early on Saturdays, I don't work then.

- ◯ haven't to
- ◯ don't have to
- ◯ don't to

e) She is a nurse so she _____ work some weekends.

- ◯ need
- ◯ need to
- ◯ needs to

5 **Complete the sentences with must, mustn't, (don't) have to, (don't) need to:**

a) The sign says "No parking". That means you _____ leave your car here.

b) There's no hurry. You _____ finish that essay until Friday of next week.

c) I'm really out of shape. I _____ start exercising regularly.

d) In Canadian schools, students _____ wear uniforms. They can wear everyday clothes.

6 **Complete with must or should.**

a) Kids _____ have their parent's permission to go online.

b) You _____ help your brother with his homework, dear. You're so smart!

c) In my school, students _____ turn off their cell phones when the classes start.

d) In my country, people _____ be 18 if they want to drive.

e) Alex, do you think I _____ wear this jacket for the concert?

f) In my opinion, all people _____ help NGOs.

67

DO NOT FORGET!

FUTURE TENSE

TO BE GOING TO
Used for predictions based on facts or ideas in the future that are concrete and sure to happen.

I am going to travel **by plane** next week. I have the tickets here with me, look.

SUBJECT + TO BE + GOING TO + VERB + COMPLEMENT.

WILL
Used for predictions based on opinions, abstract plans, promises or ideas in the future that are not concrete.

I am thinking about going to Europe next year. I will probably travel **by plane**.

SUBJECT + WILL + VERB + COMPLEMENT.

MEANS OF TRANSPORTATION
BY LAND: car, ambulance, truck, bus, bike, motorbike, train, subway, walking.
BY AIR: airplane, hot air balloon, helicopter, rocket, glider.
BY WATER: ship, sail boat, canoe, speed boat, ferry boat.

AFFIRMATIVE: I am going to travel. / I will travel.
NEGATIVE: I am not going to travel. / I (won't) travel.
INTERROGATIVE: Am I going to travel? / Will I travel?

QUESTIONS

DIRECT QUESTIONS: They are regular, objective questions that use the standard construction for interrogative sentences.

EMBEDDED QUESTIONS: They are questions that are included inside other questions or statements. They are common after introductory phrases, such as: "Do you know…?", "Can you tell me…?"

EXAMPLES
DIRECT QUESTION: Where is my **smartphone**?
INDIRECT QUESTION: Do you know where my **smartphone** is?

MODAL VERBS

SUGGESTION/ADVICE: should, ought to, had better.
OBLIGATION/NECESSITY: must, have to, need to.

LOL = laughing out loud
BRB = be right back
IDN = I don't know
IMO = in my opinion
OMG = oh my God
ASAP = as soon as possible
IDK = I don't know

TECHNOLOGIES AND PROGRAMS
Instant messaging, social networking sites, smartphone, computer, tablet, laptop, email, message app, texting, tweeting, blogs, video chat, chat rooms, forums, VoIP, emoticon.

EXAMPLES
I have a date tonight, which dress do you think I **should** wear? / You **must** turn off your cell phones. Honey, you **ought to** watch that new movie, it's fantastic! / Eric, you **had better** see a doctor, you look awful! / I **have to** study for tomorrow's test now. / People **need to** be over 18 if they want to drive.

OVERCOMING CHALLENGES

(PUC-RJ – 2000)

In the sentence *"For the first time in human history, early in the next millennium, there will be more people living in cities than on the rest of the planet"*, the future form is used to express a prediction. In which of the alternatives below is the future form used to express a similar idea?

a) Will someone help me with the luggage?

b) It will snow heavily in two days' time.

c) If it rains, the match will be cancelled.

d) Don't worry. I'll watch your dog carefully.

e) Waiter, I'll have some salad for lunch.

(JFS – 2007)

Fill in the following sentence correctly:

In my opinion, Marla _____ study harder. She _____ be approved, but she _____ improve.

a) can – could – ought

b) should – can – must

c) ought to – should – can

d) should – must – cannot

e) ought – can – must

(PUC-MG – 2004)

Recent advances in human embryology and genetic engineering have raised the issue of how this knowledge **ought to** be used, and it is now a matter of considerable public concern and debate.

The words **ought to** suggest:

a) advice.

b) ability.

c) possibility.

d) prohibition.

||| Get ready |||

1 Read some kids' games definitions and match them with the images accordingly.

a) **Blindman's buff:** a group game where a player is blindfolded and tries to catch one of the other players. ( )

b) **Fly a kite:** a game played using a light frame with a tail and designed to be flown in the air. ( )

c) **Hopscotch:** a group game where a player tosses a stone into areas of a figure drawn on the ground and hops through it and back to get the stone. ( )

d) **Hula-Hoop:** a game where the player uses a plastic toy hoop that is twirled around the body. ( )

e) **Jump-rope:** a game where the player jumps over a rope. ( )

f) **Marbles:** a game played using polished little balls made of hard material. ( )

g) **Top:** a toy designed to spin rapidly on the ground. ( )

2 Is there any traditional children's game in your country?

CHAPTER 1

Let's practice

1. Look at the comic strip below and answer the questions.

a) Why is grandma asking her grandchildren to go outside?

_____

_____

b) What kind of games does she ask her grandchildren to play?

_____

_____

c) What outdoor games did grandma mention?

_____

_____

d) Do her grandchildren know what games these are? How do you know that?

_____

e) Have you ever played any outdoor games? Which ones?

_____

_____

GLOSSARY

Kick the can: uma variação da brincadeira pega-pega.

Ghost in the graveyard: uma variação da brincadeira esconde-esconde.

Freeze tag: uma variação da brincadeira pega-pega.

Hazy: nebuloso(a).

Do you know which game it is? Match the image with the correct name from the box.

hide and seek • capture the flag • jump-rope • hand-clap • tag
blindman's buff • hopscotch • marbles • hula-hoop • fly a kite

a)

b)

c)

d)

e)

f)

g)

h)

i)

j)

Let's listen n' speak

1 Listen to Keith's memories from his childhood and put the images in order.

2 Based on what you have heard, answer.

a) How far could their kites fly?
- ( ) Not as high as they wanted.
- ( ) Extremely high.
- ( ) A little high.

b) How many boys were there? Who were they?
_____

c) What happened to their kites when they flew them too high?
_____
_____

d) One day Johnny and Stephen had a fight. What happened?
_____
_____

3 They talked about an experimental farm in the audio. Do you know what it is?

Let's practice

1) What is the sequence of the events? Number the sentences **1** or **2** in order to determine it.

a) ( ) when mom got home, ( ) she saw that I had done all my homework.

b) ( ) after they had finished playing tag, ( ) they began to play chess.

c) ( ) so he couldn't play kick the can ( ) his mom had thrown all the cans out.

d) ( ) I had not prepared my presentation well, ( ) so it was a fiasco.

e) ( ) Zach hadn't done his homework, ( ) so he did not watch TV.

2) Complete the sentences with the affirmative form of the verbs in past perfect.

a) By the time Tim found the ball to play, everyone _____ home. (to go)

b) They found the kites in a box in the attic. It _____ there forever. (to be)

c) She told me she _____ some new marbles. (to buy)

d) The kids said the teacher _____ hide and seek with them. (to play)

e) When he arrived, Eve _____ half of the pizza by herself. (to eat)

3) Circle the correct option.

a) Nobody (understood / had understood) how the kid (entered / had entered) the hollow.

b) After I (searched / had searched) for my old toys I (began / had begun) to feel nostalgic.

c) Pilar (traveled / had traveled) to Sweden before she (went / had been) to Iceland.

d) Juan (bought / had bought) some marbles before remembering his dad (bought / had bought) some for him on the previous day.

e) The children (were / had been) excited about the theater play, but the tickets (sold out / had been sold out).

LANGUAGE PIECE

Past perfect

Past perfect – actions that had already finished when another action happened.

Affirmative form

Subject pronoun + **auxiliary verb** + **main verb** + complement
                   (past tense: **had**)   (past participle)

She had left when I arrived.

4 The twins had promised to do lots of things, but they did not do them. Form negative sentences using the cues. When their mother got home, they...

a) (not do homework) ... _____

b) (not get dressed) ... _____

c) (not brush their teeth) ... _____

d) (not put away the toys) ... _____

e) (not take out the trash) ... _____

5 Join both sentences using the past perfect tense.

a) Chad finished his lunch. Then he sat down to read a book.

_____

b) Gloria played dodgeball. Before that she had a milkshake.

_____

c) I put away my marbles. Then I took a shower.

_____

d) We sorted our stamp collection. Before that we made cookies.

_____

> **TRACK 14**
>
> **Vocabulary hint**
> **Past perfect**
>
> If **had** is not completely contracted, it is usually reduced to its weak form in affirmative sentences and questions.
>
> **We had** already arrived.
> **You had** tried many times.
> **Had** they eaten?

6 Finish the sentences with your own ideas. Make all of them negative.

a) Glenn had to study hard for yesterday's test because he _____

b) I was worried she didn't arrive on time because she _____

c) Debbie didn't want to go on the school ski trip because she _____

d) We recognized Ellen at the party because she _____

LANGUAGE PIECE

Past perfect
Negative form

Subject pronoun + **auxiliary verb** + not + **main verb** + complement
(past tense: **had**)   (past participle)

(7) **Write questions using the past perfect form of the verbs.**

a) _____ him before that day? (they – to meet)

b) _____ this game before today? (you – to see)

c) _____ a championship before now? (we – to win)

d) _____ these stickers before today? (he – to buy)

(8) **Complete the questions with the past perfect. Then match them to the correct answers.**

a) Brazil held the Olympic Games in 2016. _____ them before? (it – to hold)

b) When Stephen King wrote the book Carrie, how many books _____ before? (he – to publish)

c) When the Germans elected Angela Merkel as First Chancellor, _____ a woman before? (they – to elect)

d) Terry was feeling a very painful stomach ache. _____ before? (he – to feel)

- ( ) None.

- ( ) No, they hadn't.

- ( ) No, he hadn't.

- ( ) No, it had not.

(9) **Circle the correct option.**

a) What (had you done / had you do) before you left home this morning?

b) When (had you last wrote / had you last written) in English before now?

c) How many times (had you study / had you studied) the past perfect before today?

d) (Had you use / Had you used) this pen/pencil before?

e) Who (had you talked / had you talk) to when the teacher arrived for the first class?

> **LANGUAGE PIECE**
>
> **Past perfect**
> **Interrogative form**
> **Auxiliary verb** + subject pronoun + **main verb** + complement
> (past tense: **had**)   (past participle)

Let's listen n' speak

1. Pablo and Mat are in the garage looking for a baseball bat, but they end up finding other things. Listen to their conversation and say who said what. Use **P** (Pablo) or **M** (Matt) to label the sentences.

a) ◯ Check this out!

b) ◯ My sister got this for Christmas.

c) ◯ We got desperate to watch Spy Kids.

d) ◯ My sister wanted the popcorn.

e) ◯ The tickets had been sold out.

2. Read the sentences and rewrite them correcting their mistakes.

a) They found a PS3 in the old things.
_____

b) Pablo's dad took them to the cinema on the first day.
_____

c) Pablo's sister wanted ice-cream.
_____

d) Leo had told them the beginning of the movie story.
_____

3. Choose the correct option to complete each sentence.

a) Pablo found a _____
   • ◯ CD player   • ◯ CD

b) The game they found is called _____
   • ◯ cat's crib   • ◯ cat's cradle

c) Pablo's dad _____ the wallet at home.
   • ◯ had forgotten   • ◯ had lost

d) Pablo was _____ Leo.
   • ◯ nice to   • ◯ angry at

4. Pair up and talk to your partner about things you used to do in the past. Follow the example.

• **Had** you **watched** Avatar when you turned 12?
Yes, I had. / No, I had not.

Chapter 3: Let's read n' write

A BRIEF HISTORY OF TOYS

Dating from the 16th century, the word 'toy' designated objects used as **playthings** and **amusements** for adults.

EARLY TOYS
Dating from 4000 BC, the earliest known toy are the small stones, **clay** balls or **marbles**. From medieval times, there are yo-yos, cup, and ball toys, usually made of wood.

18TH CENTURY
Most toys were originated in the late 18th century, including dolls, **hobbyhorses**, stick horses, and kites.

19TH CENTURY
Due to technological advances, **jigsaw puzzles** were manufactured and seen as an educational **pastime**, often **featuring** historic figures such as kings and queens.
In the 1820s, games like dominoes, playing cards, and **teetotums** were popular.
In the 1840s, toy trains appeared.
In the 1870s, more educational games, like abacuses, were produced.
In the 1880s, with the Industrial Revolution, the **mass-produced** toys appeared.

EARLY 20TH CENTURY
More elaborate toys began to be produced, such as the toy car, and the "Teddy bears" became a synonymous with toy bears worldwide.
Due to the World War I, a good variety of toys reflecting the conflict appeared, such as toy soldiers.
In the 1920s and 1930s, the characters Felix The Cat and Mickey Mouse appeared and these toy **figures** began to be produced and **merchandised** worldwide.

MID-20TH CENTURY
Due to the World War II, toys were made from cheaper materials (card or paper), such as **cut out** paper dolls.
In the 1950s, television programs became the **entertainment** source with programs like Muffin the Mule and Sooty.
In the 1960s, when the man walked on the Moon for the first time, a variety of space toys appeared, such as the lunar space buggy.
In the 1970s, the first interactive TV game was produced.
In the 1990s, the first **portable** video game system was produced and called Gameboy.

21ST CENTURY
At the beginning of this millennium, many **souvenir** toys were produced, such as the Beanie Baby bear. The popularity of electronic toys continued to increase with toys like virtual pet tamagotchis and micropets.
Nowadays, there are a handful of toys that are **geared** to be sophisticated and tech-oriented in ways to **infuse** intelligence, social causes and technology.

GLOSSARY
Amusements: divertimentos.
Clay: argila.
Cut out (to cut out): recortado (recortar).
Entertainment: entretenimento.
Featuring (to feature): apresentando (apresentar).
Figures: figuras.
Geared (to gear): equipado (equipar).
Hobbyhorses: cavalinhos de madeira.
Infuse (to infuse): infundir, inspirar.
Jigsaw puzzles: quebra-cabeças.
Marbles: bolinhas de gude.
Mass-produced: produzido em massa.
Merchandised (to merchandise): comercializado (comercializar).
Pastime: passatempo.
Playthings: brinquedos.
Portable: portátil.
Souvenir: lembrancinha.
Teetotums: piorra (brinquedo parecido com o pião).

Based on: *Toy Timeline*, available at: <https://brightonmuseums.org.uk/discover/2012/05/21/toy-timeline/>; *Play through the ages*, available at: <www.thegeniusofplay.org/genius/time/toy-timeline.aspx> Access: Aug. 2018.

1 **Answer according to the infographic.**

a) When was the word "toy" first used?
_____

b) What were the first toys? When did they appear?
_____

c) When did the hobbyhorses and kites appear?
_____

d) What was merchandised worldwide?
_____

e) What was the theme of the first jigsaw puzzles? How were they seen?
_____
_____

f) When was the first interactive TV game produced?
_____

g) What toy became a synonymous with toy bears worldwide? When did it appear?
_____
_____

h) When was the first portable video game system produced? What was its name?
_____
_____

i) What kind of toy continued to increase its popularity in the 21st Century? Give examples.
_____
_____

j) What kind of toys are produced nowadays? What do they infuse?
_____
_____

2 **Think about the text and its characteristics and answer the questions.**

a) What kind of text is it?

- ○ Narrative.
- ○ Descriptive.
- ○ Informative.
- ○ Short.
- ○ Medium.
- ○ Long.

b) What is the aim of the text?

_____

c) What kind of language is used in it?

_____

d) What elements are part of this type of text?

_____

_____

e) What kind of text is an infographic? What information does it bring? Check all that apply.

- ○ Empirical facts.
- ○ Data.
- ○ Descriptive.
- ○ Informative.
- ○ Hypothetical facts.
- ○ Persuasive.

f) Where can texts like this be found?

_____

3 **Now, create a guide in an infographic form about the Brazilian childhood toys and games. Use the following briefing to help you out.**

- Organize yourselves into 5 groups. Each group will research about a different Brazilian region.
- Research about the main childhood toys and games of your group's designated region.
- Make a list with images and all the information you can find about these toys and games.
- Gather data from reliable sources.
- Write a draft of the infographic and make a peer evaluation of it with your classmates.
- Write a new version of the infographic, making all the necessary adjustments.
- Expose the infographics in class, presenting it to your classmates.

81

CHAPTER 4

||| Citizenship moment |||

RIGHTS OF THE CHILD
adds'água

Children's rights are listed in the UN Convention on the Rights of the Child and most of the countries have agreed to them. All these rights are connected to each other, and are equally important. Here it goes a **summary** of them.

Article 1 and 2 – Everyone under 18 has these rights, no matter who they are, where they live, what their language, religion, **gender**, or culture is, **whether** they have a **disability** or if they are rich or poor. No child should be treated **unfairly** on any basis.

Article 3 to 5 – The right to be **taken into account** in all adults' decisions. The government and families must make sure their rights are protected and provide an environment where they can grow and reach their potential.

Article 6 to 8 – The right to be alive and to have a name that should be officially recognized, as well as the right to have an identity and a nationality.

Article 9 to 11 – The right to live with their parent(s), and with a family who cares for them.

Article 11 – The right to be protected from **kidnapping**.

Article 12 to 15 – The right to give their opinion, to find out things, and share what they think with others, by talking, drawing, writing, or in any other way unless it **harms** or offends other people. The right to choose their own religion and **beliefs**, as well as to choose their own friends and join or **set up** groups, as long as it isn't harmful to others.

Article 16 – The right to privacy.

Article 17 – The right to get and understand information that is important to their well-being, from any available source, as long as they are not harmful.

Article 18 to 23 – The right **to be raised** by their parent(s) – if possible – and to be protected from being hurt and **mistreated**, in body or mind. The right to special care and help if they cannot live with their parents, if adopted or in **foster care**, if they are a **refugee**, or have a disability.

Article 24 to 29 – The right to the best **health care** possible, safe water to drink, nutritious food, **clothing**, a clean and safe environment, good quality education, and to have their basic needs met. The right to get help from the government if poor or in need.

Article 30 to 37 – The right to practice their own culture, language, and religion; to play and rest; to be protected from harmful work; to be safe and paid **fairly**. The right to be protected from drugs, sexual abuse, kidnaping, or any kind of **exploitation** or punishment in a cruel or harmful way.

Article 38 to 41 – The right to protection and freedom from war, and to get help if hurt, neglected or badly treated. The right to legal help and fair treatment in the justice system.

Article 42 – The right to know their rights.

Articles 43 to 54 – The right to have access to governments and international organizations that work to **ensure** children are protected with their rights.

Cristiane Viana

GLOSSARY

Beliefs: crenças.
Clothing: vestimenta.
Disability: deficiência.
Ensure (to ensure): garantir.
Exploitation: exploração.
Fairly: justamente.
Foster care: sistema de acolhimento.
Gender: gênero.
Harms (to harm): prejudica (prejudicar).
Health care: sistema de saúde.
Kidnapping: sequestro.
Mistreated: maltratado.
Refugee: refugiado.
Set up (to set up): configurar.
Summary: resumo.
Taken into account (to take into account): levado em consideração (levar em consideração).
To be raised: ser criado.
Unfairly: injustamente.
Whether: se.

Based on: <www.unicef.org/rightsite/files/uncrcchilldfriendlylanguage.pdf>. Access: Aug. 2018.

Let's practice

1 **Say if the statement is T (true) or F (false).**

a) ◯ All children under 18 are entitled to the Rights of Child.

b) ◯ Children must be treated differently depending on their race, gender, religion or nationality.

c) ◯ Every child has the right to have an identity and nationality.

d) ◯ No child has the right to give their opinion, to share their beliefs, or to have privacy.

e) ◯ Some children cannot be protected from being hurt and mistreated.

f) ◯ Children's rights are protected by law.

g) ◯ Children do not have the right to get help from the government if poor or in need.

h) ◯ Children have the right to have a safe place to live.

> **EXPLORING**
>
> Humanium
> - www.humanium.org/en/child-rights/
>
> Children & Young People's Commissioner Scotland
> - www.cypcs.org.uk/rights/picture
>
> Cartoons for Children's Rights
> - www.unicef.org/crcartoons/
>
> **EXPLORING**
> - *The history of toys: from spinning tops to robots*, by Deborah Jaffe. (The History of Press Ltd.).

2 Now, rewrite the false statements from the previous exercise, so that they are true.

_____

_____

_____

_____

3 In your opinion, what are the four most important rights listed on the infographic? List them on your notebook and explain the reasons why you chose them.

> **PROJECT**
>
> **Research: ECA**
>
> Have you ever heard about Estatuto da Criança e do Adolescente (ECA)? Form small groups and research about ECA: its history, its articles, who fiscalizes it, etc. Once you gather all the information, prepare a summary with all the main data about it and discuss it with your classmates.

83

UNIT 6
HOW MUCH HAVE OUR LIVES CHANGED?

||| Get ready |||

1 Have you ever seen any of these objects before?

2 Can you name them?

> camera • carriage • gas lamp
> gramophone • telephone • typewriter

3 Do you know anyone who has used any of these objects or has any of them?

4 Are any of these machines used nowadays?

5 Which gadgets represent the evolution to each one of the following objects? Match.

- **a)** Gas lamp.
- **b)** Typewriter.
- **c)** Gramophone.
- **d)** Camera.
- **e)** Carriage.
- **f)** Telephone.

- Smartphone.
- Car.
- Digital camera.
- Digital Music Player.
- Computer.
- Lamp bulb / Electric energy.

Let's practice

1 Let's talk about technology. Answer the questions with your classmates.

a) Have you ever thought what it was like to live in the past? Did people have the same technology we have today?

b) What kind of things do we have today that people didn't have in the beginning of the 20th century? Name some of them.

c) Do you think the evolution of technology has been good to people? Why (not)?

d) Can you think of 5 ways technology has evolued since the past century (1900s)?

e) What about the means of communication? How much have they evolved?

f) Explain with 2 or 3 examples how our lives would be if technology had not evolued this much.

2 How do you think these means of communication differ from each other? Think about the advantages and disadvantages of each one.

Means of communication	Advantages	Disadvantages
Face-to-face		
Telephone		
Letter		
Email		
Instant message		

3 Considering the current way people communicate and the technological advances, how do you imagine the future of the means of communication?

_____

_____

_____

4 Which words are used with each one of these verbs? Complete the table with the words from the box.

> a bomb • a list • bikes • crops • dinner • housework
> laundry • mail • money • research • the bed • TV sets

Make	Assemble	Sort	Do

Now, add two more items to each category of the table above.

5 Which of the following activities are done by humans? And by machines?

> assemble • manufacture • produce • sell • sort • use

Machines	Humans

a) Name three other activities done by humans and three by machines.

_____

_____

_____

b) Make a list of three modern machines you have at home and describe the task each one performs.

_____

_____

_____

_____

Let's listen n' speak

1) When we think about the past and the present, we realize that a lot has changed, and many things that we take for granted today have actually revolutionized human lifestyle. Can you think of some of these things?

_____

2) Going back in the past even more, have you ever imagined your life without basic things like the wheel? How would that be? Discuss with your classmates.

3) Let's find out a little bit more about the wheel invention. Listen carefully.

a) Who were the first ones to use the wheels?

_____

_____

b) Why is the creation of the wheel the most significant discovery?

_____

_____

c) Were wheels in the past the same we have today?

_____

d) In your opinion, what could have happened if the wheels had not been invented?

_____

_____

e) After listening to the audio, think about its first statement: "We cannot imagine our lives without any kind of movement". Can you think of how life would be without the wheel? How would people go from one place to another?

_____

_____

Let's practice

1 Say if the following sentences are in the **A** (active) or **P** (passive) voice.

a) ( ) An atomic bomb is made up of uranium.

b) ( ) Scientists are paid good money.

c) ( ) They build weapons.

d) ( ) Cell phones are used every day.

e) ( ) Social media connects people worldwide.

2 Circle the correct option.

a) 43% of the lithium in the world (is find / is found) in Salar de Uyuni, in Bolivia.

b) Superbugs (are creating / are created) by bacteria that have become resistant to antibiotics.

c) Is 3D printing a process in which material (is joined / are joined) or solidified together under computer control?

d) 3.4 gigawatts of wind energy (is produced / are produced) in the 127 wind farms in the state of Rio Grande do Norte.

e) Solar energy (is transforming / is transformed) to be used in homes.

3 Complete the following sentences using the simple present form of the passive voice.

a) A photovoltaic system _____ of an array of photovoltaic modules, an inverter, a battery pack for storage, and interconnection wiring. (to make up)

b) Your credit card info _____ in your app *Wallet* and then your smartphone _____ to pay for things through it. (to store / to use)

c) Your items _____ by barcode readers in self checkouts at supermarkets. (to scan)

d) The Fairphone 2, one of the few green options in the market of smartphones, _____ from recycled plastic and aluminum. (to make)

LANGUAGE PIECE

Passive voice (present)

Affirmative

Subject pronoun + verb to be (present) + main verb (past participle) + complement.

Negative

Subject pronoun + verb to be (present) + not + main verb (past participle) + complement.

Interrogative

Verb to be (present) + subject pronoun + main verb (past participle) + complement?

4 Unscramble the words and form sentences in the passive voice.

a) in Germany / was / the first car / in 1886 / built

_____

_____

b) in 1967/ was / in the USA / the / microwave oven / used / first

_____

_____

c) was / the penicillin / discovered / by Dr. Alexander Fleming

_____

_____

d) Marie Curie / radium / were / polonium / discovered / by / and

_____

> **LANGUAGE PIECE**
>
> **Passive voice (past)**
>
> **Affirmative**
>
> **Subject pronoun** + **verb to be** (past) + **main verb** (past participle) + complement.
>
> **Negative**
>
> **Subject pronoun** + **verb to be** (past) + **not** + **main verb** (past participle) + complement.
>
> **Interrogative**
>
> **Verb to be** (past) + **subject pronoun** + **main verb** (past participle) + complement?

5 Complete the sentences with the correct form of the verb to be in the past tense.

a) The first TV set _____ sold in 1928.

b) Thousands of tons of napalm _____ dropped in Vietnam, from 1963 to 1973.

c) The iPod _____ launched and supersonic planes _____ developed in the twentieth century.

6 Rewrite the sentences in the passive voice.

a) The British invented the steam engine.

_____

b) The Chinese invented gunpowder in the 9th century.

_____

c) Hugh Locke-King designed the motor racing circuit in 1907.

_____

d) James Watson and Francis Crick discovered the structure of DNA.

_____

7 Write if the sentence is in the **PR** (passive present) or **PA** (passive past).

a) ( ) An atomic bomb is made up of uranium.

b) ( ) Scientists were paid good money.

c) ( ) Weapons are sold worldwide.

d) ( ) Cell phones are used every day.

e) ( ) The first underground system was built in London.

8 Check the correct options.

a) ( ) I sent a birthday card to my grandma last week.

( ) I was sent a birthday card to my grandma last week.

b) ( ) Three people hurt in the accident yesterday.

( ) Three people were hurt in the accident yesterday.

c) ( ) He contacted by the boss in 2011.

( ) He was contacted by the boss in 2011.

d) ( ) My office robbed last week, but fortunately the police caught the thief.

( ) My office was robbed last week, but fortunately the police caught the thief.

9 Write questions in the passive voice using the given information.

a) when – first vaccine for smallpox – to invent

_____

b) What – optical fibers – to use

_____

c) Who – the telephone – to invent

_____

d) How much – Nissan Leaf – to sell – in the USA for

_____

e) Where – artificial artery – to create

_____

> **TRACK 17**
>
> **Vocabulary hint**
> **The passive voice focuses on the action rather than on the doer or agent of it.**
>
> Robots drive cars. ⟶ Cars are driven by robots.
>
> Robots drove cars. ⟶ Cars were driven by robots.
>
> Robots are driving cars. ⟶ Cars are being driven by robots.
>
> Robots were driving cars. ⟶ Cars were being driven by robots.

Let's listen n' speak

1 Carlo and his cousin Marcy are taking a quiz. Listen to the dialogue and write down Marcy's answers.

a) Where in the USA is the Silicon Valley located?

_____

b) When was the first human-to-human heart transplant performed?

- ( ) 1975
- ( ) 1967

c) What was discovered by a scientist during an experience that originated Teflon™?

- ( ) A polymer.
- ( ) A gas.

d) What are nanobots?

_____

e) What other institutions are said to develop nanobots?

_____

f) How was the airplane that Santos Dumont invented called?

_____

2 Choose the correct option.

a) The Silicon Valley is in (San Antonio / San Francisco).

b) The first heart transplant happened in (South Africa / South Asia).

c) Teflon™ was invented (by accident / on purpose).

d) Nanobots are developed at (hospitals / research labs).

e) In 1906, 14 Bis was invented by a (South African / South American).

3 Research and answer the questions.

a) Is Silicon Valley a company?

_____

_____

b) Where in South Africa was the heart transplant performed? _____

c) When was Teflon™ invented? _____

Let's read n' write

Tecnology

Disruptive Technology

Margaret Rouse

A disruptive technology is one that **displaces** an established technology and **shakes up** the industry or a **ground-breaking** product that creates a completely new industry.

Harvard Business School professor Clayton M. Christensen coined the term disruptive technology. In his 1997 best-selling book, "The Innovator's Dilemma," Christensen separates new technology into two categories: sustaining and disruptive. Sustaining technology relies on incremental improvements to an already established technology. Disruptive technology lacks refinement, often has performance problems because it is new, appeals to a limited audience and may not yet have a proven practical application. (Such was the case with Alexander Graham Bell's "electrical speech machine," which we now call the telephone.)

Here are a few examples of disruptive technologies:

- The personal computer (PC) **displaced** the typewriter and forever changed the way we work and communicate.
- The Windows operating system's combination of **affordability** and a **user-friendly** interface was instrumental in the rapid development of the personal computing industry in the 1990s. Personal computing disrupted the television industry, as well as a great number of other activities.
- Email transformed the way we communicating, largely displacing letter-writing and disrupting the postal and greeting card industries.
- Cell phones made it possible for people to call us anywhere and disrupted the **telecom** industry.
- The laptop computer and mobile computing made a mobile **workforce** possible and made it possible for people to connect to corporate networks and collaborate from anywhere. In many organizations, laptops replaced desktops.
- Smartphones largely replaced cell phones and **PDAs** and, because of the available apps, also disrupted: pocket cameras, MP3 players, calculators and GPS devices, among many other possibilities. For some mobile users, smartphones often replace laptops. Others prefer a tablet.

GLOSSARY

Affordability: acessibilidade (financeira).

Displaced (to displace): deslocado (deslocar).

Displaces (to displace): desloca (deslocar).

Ground-breaking: inovador.

PDAs (Personal Digital Assistants): assistentes pessoais digitais.

Shakes up (to shake up): sacode (sacudir).

Telecom: telecomunicação.

User-friendly: simples, intuitivo, acessível.

Workforce: trabalhadores.

Tecnology

- **Cloud computing** has been a hugely disruptive technology in the business world, displacing many resources that would conventionally have been located in-house or provided as a traditionally hosted service.
- **Social networking** has had a major impact on the way we communicate and – especially for personal use – has disrupted telephone, email, instant messaging and event planning. […]

Margaret Rouse. *Disruptive Technology*. Available at: <https://whatis.techtarget.com/definition/disruptive-technology>. Access: Aug. 2018.

1 After reading the article, answer the following questions.

a) What is the definition of "disruptive technology"?
_____
_____
_____

b) What are the cons of disruptive technology mentioned in the text?
_____
_____
_____

c) When and by whom was the term "disruptive technology" first mentioned?
_____

d) What is the definition of "sustaining technology"?
_____

e) What example of past invention considered a disruptive technology is mentioned in the text?
_____

f) What late technologies did the following ones replace?

- Smartphones _____
_____

- Cloud computing _____

- Social networking _____

2 Analyze the text and answer.

a) What kind of text is it?
_____

b) What kind of information does it present?
_____

c) What is the purpose of the text?
_____
_____

d) What kind of language is used in it?
_____
_____

e) Where can texts like this be found?
_____
_____

f) What elements are part of this type of text?
_____
_____
_____

3 Let's create an informative article explaining Artificial Intelligence (AI). Follow the instructions.

- Research Artificial Intelligence (AI) on reliable sources and by trustworthy authorities on the subject.
- Write a draft of your article and make a peer evaluation of it with your classmates.
- Write a new version of the article, making all the necessary adjustments.
- Hand in your article to your teacher.

▶️ **EXPLORING**
- *Rogue One: A Star Wars story* (2016)
- *Passengers* (2016)
- *Chappie* (2015)
- *Tron – Legacy* (2010)

📖 **EXPLORING**
The way things work now, by David Macaulay (HMH Books for Young Readers)

||| Tying in |||

Culture and Society

Cross Cultural Awareness and Communication

[...] What is culture?

Culture is the integrated pattern of human behaviour that includes thoughts, communication, actions, <u>customs</u>, beliefs, values and institutions of a racial, ethnic, religious or social group. It reflects the norms and values of a given society and constitutes, to a large extent, the way in which individuals in that society views the world.

Some of the elements of culture include: language; dress and appearance; food and eating habits; music and dance; time and time-consciousness; interpersonal relationships; and, beliefs and attitudes. Some other definitions that are useful when considering cultural difference include:

• **<u>Acculturation</u>** – the process of adapting to or adopting a different culture.
• **Ethnic** – refers to membership of a group linked by race, nationality, language or a common cultural heritage.
• **Race** – a socially defined population that is derived from distinguishable physical characteristics.
• **Stereotype** – the notion that all people from a given group are the same. [...]

Why is communicating across cultures so difficult?

More than 80% of the world's people live in societies that are collectivist in nature. Those living in <u>Western</u> societies live in societies that are individualist in nature. This is a fundamental difference that has the potential to create constant <u>misunderstanding</u> and, therefore, <u>miscommunication</u>. [...] Remembering that we are all human beings driven by the same emotions, instincts and ambitions may also help us to see cultural difference as something that is on the surface and not so <u>threatening</u>.

Useful tips for communicating across cultures

[...]
• Be complete, explicit and pay attention to the other person's response.
• Be alert for different meanings.
• Avoid metaphors, colloquialisms and jargon. [...]
• Acknowledge cultural differences without <u>bias</u> and be persistent. [...]
• Do not ask questions that you would not or could not answer yourself.

Student Centre UTAS. *Cross Cultural Awareness and Communication*. Available at: <http://www.utas.edu.au/__data/assets/pdf_file/0018/11538/Cross-Cultural-Awareness.pdf>. Access: Aug. 2018.

GLOSSARY

Acculturation: aculturação.

Bias: distorção de julgamento; viés.

Customs: costumes.

Miscommunication: falta de comunicação.

Misunderstanding: mal-entendido.

Threatening: ameaçador.

Western: ocidental.

Let's practice

1 What patterns of human behavior does culture include?

_____
_____
_____
_____

PROJECT

Classroom communication system
Organize yourselves into small groups and think about a communication system to be used in your classroom by you and your classmates. Be creative and try to think of ways of being either revolutionary or social and culture-friendly.

2 What other elements does culture embrace?

_____
_____
_____

3 What terms do these definitions belong to? Match.

acculturation • ethnic • race • stereotype

a) A socially defined population perceived with the same physical characteristics. _____

b) The notion of all people from a certain group as having the same traits. _____

c) The process of adjusting to or embracing a different culture. _____

d) Being part of a group linked by a common race, nationality, language, or cultural heritage. _____

4 What is the fundamental difference that causes misunderstandings and miscommunications among people?

_____
_____
_____

5 What can help people to see cultural differences as something not to be afraid of?

_____
_____
_____

97

REVIEW

1. Write sentences in the past perfect using the clues.

a) the kids – to organize their desks (negative)

_____

b) Mary – to set the marbles (affirmative)

_____

c) Paul – to open the windows (interrogative)

_____

2. Read the following paragraph and write sentences in the past perfect.

> George and Fred started the day playing Mario Bros. games. Then, they rode their bikes. After that, they came home for lunch. Then, they played Uno. After that, they jumped rope. Then, they watched SpongeBob.

a) _____

b) _____

c) _____

d) _____

e) _____

3. Match the correct parts of the sentences.

a) Kevin failed his exam because

b) Mel was allowed to have a sleepover party

c) Had Jim gotten upset because

d) Max did not buy playdough because

e) Had Lea ever solved a Rubik's Cube

• ( ) before that day?

• ( ) he didn't win the bets tournament?

• ( ) he had spent his money on stickers.

• ( ) because she had done all her week tasks well.

• ( ) he had not reviewed the texts.

98

4 Write six questions in the passive voice, three in the present and three in the past tense.

_____

_____

_____

_____

_____

_____

5 Rewrite the sentences in the passive voice.

a) I posted a photo on Facebook.

_____

b) Google tracked my recent purchases.

_____

c) Electric vehicles produce zero pollution.

_____

d) Most Swedes do not carry cash with them.

_____

e) Steptoe and Edwards carried out the first in vitro fertilization in 1977.

_____

6 Write if the sentences are **R** (right) or **W** (wrong).

a) ( ) Gagarin were the first human sent to space, in 1961.

b) ( ) The London underground was the first one ever built.

c) ( ) Gold is shown as Au on the periodic table.

d) ( ) The Great Wall were built over a period of 200 years.

e) ( ) 1 million tons of electronic waste are produced in Brazil every year.

DO NOT FORGET!

PAST PERFECT

We use the **PAST PERFECT** when we are already talking about the past and want to talk about an earlier past time. We can use it in narratives or in reported speeches.

NARRATIVE

AFF: When his mom arrived, he had already eaten all the candy. (First the kid ate the candy, and then his mom arrived.)

INT: Had he eaten all the candy when his mom arrived?

NEG: When his mom arrived, he had not (hadn't) eaten all the candy yet.

REPORTED SPEECH

AFF: They told her they had visited the Louvre before. (First they visited the Louvre, and then they told her that.)

INT: Had they visited the Louvre before?

NEG: They told her they had not (hadn't) visited the Louvre before.

ACTIVE VOICE AND PASSIVE VOICE

ACTIVE VOICE

It's when the subject performs the action denoted by the verb.

AFF: John cleans the room.

John did all the exercises.

INT: Does John clean the room?

Did John do all the exercises?

NEG: John does not clean the room.

John did not do all the exercises.

PASSIVE VOICE

It's when the subject is being acted upon by the verb.

AFF: The room is cleaned by John.

All the exercises were done by John.

INT: Is the room cleaned by John?

Were all the exercises done by John?

NEG: The room isn't cleaned by John.

All the exercises weren't done by John.

OVERCOMING CHALLENGES

(UNB – 2013)

The man's decision to take up woodworking happened at an indefinite time in the past.

- ( ) right
- ( ) wrong

(CEFET – 2007)

> Most people know what an iPod is, but what does this word mean? According to one theory, it's an acronym for "Interface Protocol Option Devices". According to another, "i" stands for "internet", while Pod stands for "portable device".
> A pod also refers to a container provided by nature: peas grow in a pod, and an iPod contains music. Podcasting, on the other hand, is a variation of broadcasting. Now you can download programs from the internet onto your iPod, instead of listening to them on the radio.
>
> (Speak Up, nº 231)

De acordo com o texto,

a) ( ) o iPod, segundo mais de uma teoria, é um invólucro natural.

b) ( ) o iPod, de acordo com mais de uma teoria, é um anacronismo.

c) ( ) o iPod é algo conhecido pela maioria das pessoas.

d) ( ) a internet permitiu a criação, ainda que teórica, de uma variante de gravador de músicas.

e) ( ) o iPod, um aparelho portátil, pode ser usado como internet.

UNIT 7
WHAT IF THE STORIES WERE TRUE?

Zeus, Greek god of sky and ruler of the Olympia gods.

Thor, Nordic god of sky and thunder.

Isis, Egyptian goddess of rebirth.

Tupã, Brazilian god creation and light.

||| Get ready |||

1 What do the images represent?
- ◯ Mythological figures.
- ◯ Historical figures.

2 What is the purpose of a myth?

_____
_____

3 What myths or mythical characters do you know? Make a list and compare your answers to see who knows the most.

_____
_____
_____

4 Look at the images again. In pairs, discuss what you know about each of them.

Subrahmanya, Hindu god of war.

Schichifukujin takarabun, Japanese seven gods of fortune.

Let's practice

1 Let's find out more about myths. Read the text below and answer the questions.

Curiosities

What is a Myth?

Myths deal with **ancient** stories, such as the adventures of the Greek gods. Mythology is a collection of traditional stories that express the **beliefs** or values of a group of people. The stories often focus on human qualities such as good and evil. […]

Available at: <www.kidsinco.com/myth/>. Access: Aug. 2018.

Myth

A myth is a traditional story, which may describe the origins of the world and/or of a people. A myth is an **attempt** to explain mysteries, supernatural events, and cultural traditions. Sometimes sacred in nature, a myth can involve gods or other creatures. […]

Available at: <http://classiclit.about.com/cs/10th14thcentury/a/aa_definemyth.htm>. Access: Aug. 2018.

GLOSSARY
Ancient: antigos(as).
Attempt: tentativa.
Beliefs: crenças.

a) Explain what you understood about myths.

_____

_____

_____

b) Check all that apply. A myth…

- ◯ …is a traditional story.
- ◯ …is a historical fact.
- ◯ …expresses beliefs and values.
- ◯ …is the same for every culture.
- ◯ …isn't a cultural tradition.
- ◯ …is a story about evil and good.
- ◯ …is about gods and supernatural creatures.
- ◯ …is about everyday life.

2 What do you know about these mythological figures? Match the sentences and the images.

- ◯
- ◯
- ◯
- ◯

a) If you answer her question incorrectly, she will eat you.

b) If you look at her, you will turn into stone.

c) If you destroy nature, he will punish you.

d) If you hear her singing, you will end up at the bottom of the river.

3 Look at the sentences below and answer.

| **I.** If you destroy nature, he will punish you. | **II.** If you look at her, you will turn into stone. |

a) Which verb tenses are used in the sentences?
- ◯ Present.
- ◯ Past.
- ◯ Future.

b) What do these sentences mean?
- ◯ Cause and consequence of something.
- ◯ The reason for some happening.

c) Can you tell which part of the following sentences is the cause and which is the consequence?

- If Pandora opens the box, bad things will happen.

Cause: _____

Consequence: _____

- Saci will trick you if you take the medicinal plants from the forest without permission.

Cause: _____

Consequence: _____

Let's listen n' speak

1 Listen to a radio program about the Greek myth of Hercules and the animated movie and tell if the sentences are about the **M** (myth) or the **A** (animation).

a) ◯ Hercules was the son of the god Zeus and goddess Hera.

b) ◯ Hercules was the son of the god Zeus and a mortal.

c) ◯ Hercules was born a god, but became a semi-god because of a potion.

d) ◯ Hercules was born a semi-god, a mortal with god-like strength.

e) ◯ Hercules became a god after performing the 12 heroic labors.

f) ◯ Hercules became a god after proving himself a true hero on Earth.

2 Are the stories in the animated movie and in the Greek myth the same? Can we consider the animated story an accurate version?

_____

_____

_____

3 Listen to the radio program again and try to match the expressions to their correct meanin. You can use a dictionary to help you out.

> background • godlike • to kidnap
> to strip out • wrath

a) _____: the general situation in which something happens; a type of family or culture someone comes from.

b) _____: better or more impressive than an ordinary human being.

c) _____: very great anger.

d) _____: to remove or take off; to deprive of possessions.

e) _____: illegally take someone away and make them a prisoner.

Let's practice

1) Match the columns to form sentences.

a) If you lend me some money,
b) If Lily comes to Canada,
c) If the children don't arrive on time,
d) If we take Rose to the show,
e) If the students tell us what they need,

( ) we will be able to help them.
( ) they will miss the school bus.
( ) she will see her favorite band for the first time.
( ) I will be able to buy the tickets to the concert.
( ) she will practice her English.

2) Circle the correct words to complete the sentences:

a) The teacher (will be / is) happy if all students (did / do) their homework.
b) If it (can't / rains) this afternoon, we (would / will) have a lazy day at home.
c) Maddy (will come / comes) to the party if she (doesn't / isn't) have to work on Saturday.
d) If we (will work / work) together, we (finish / will finish) this paper in time to watch the game.

LANGUAGE PIECE

First conditional

If + **subject pronoun** + **verb** (**simple present**) + complement,
+ **subject pronoun** + **auxiliary verb** (**will**) + **main verb** (**infinitive**) + complement.

If you read a lot, **you will improve** your vocabulary.

3) Write sentences using the given prompts.

a) wake up late / miss bus

___

b) miss bus / lose job

___

c) lose job / not have money

___

d) not have money / lose home

___

e) lose home / not have place to live

___

107

4 Use the cues to ask questions in the first conditional.

a) If go Canada / take a picture in Niagara Falls.

_____

_____

b) If meet Rose / tell her the test is tomorrow.

_____

_____

c) If learn how to drive / give me a ride to school.

_____

_____

d) If get a job / buy a new computer.

_____

_____

> **Vocabulary hint**
> **First Conditional – order of clauses**
>
> **If-clause + main clause –** There is a pause between clauses:
>
> If you read a lot, your vocabulary will improve.
>
> **Will clause – if-clause –** There is no pause between clauses:
>
> Your vocabulary will improve if you read a lot.

5 Rewrite the sentences in order to make them correct by using the first conditional.

a) If we not hurry, we won't be on time.

_____

_____

b) If we will recycle more, we will help to save the planet.

_____

_____

c) What do you do if you don't have any homework today?

_____

_____

d) If we not stop global warming, many species will die out.

_____

_____

6 Board game. Team up, follow your teacher's instructions and have fun.

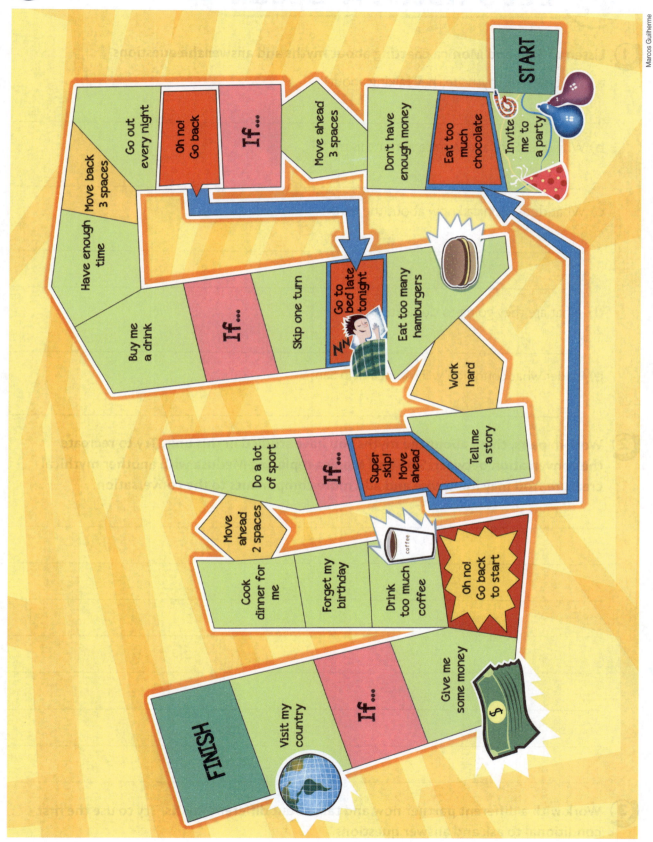

Let's listen n' speak

1) Listen to Sam and Monica chatting about myths and answer the questions.

a) Which Greek myth are they talking about?
_____

b) Why does Sam ask Monica about this myth?
_____

c) What does Monica know about the myth?
_____
_____

d) What are they going to do next?
_____

e) Under what condition will Monica help Sam?
_____

2) Work in pairs, think about the myths you have studied in this unit. Try to recreate the conversation between Sam and Monica replacing Medusa with another mythical creature. You may improvise and add more components to the conversation.

_____
_____
_____
_____
_____
_____
_____

3) Work with a different partner now and talk about different myths. Try to use the first conditional to ask and answer questions.

Let's read n' write

1. Have you ever heard the story of King Midas? This is an adaptation of the story into a movie script. Read it and answer the questions.

Theater

King Midas Script

- **Characters:** Narrator, Midas, Wizard, Daughter.
- **Setting:** King Midas' castle, Wizard's cottage, River.
- Script

Scene 1 – Wizard's cottage

NARRATOR: *Once upon a time there was a very kind king called Midas. His only fault was to want to have all the gold in the world.*

MIDAS: *Gold is more important to me than anything else in the world.*

NARRATOR: *One day he did a favor to a god.*

WIZARD: *Thank you for your favor, king Midas. In **acknowledgment** I will **grant** you anything you wish.*

MIDAS: *I wish that everything I touch turns into gold.*

WIZARD: *Your wish is foolish, Midas, and it can get you into a lot of trouble.*

MIDAS: *I don't agree. That's the only thing I want.*

WIZARD: *Very well. Your wish will come true.*

NARRATOR: *And so it happened. Everything king Midas touched turned into gold: his clothes, his castle, his food, everything. Till one day, his daughter said to him:*

Scene 2 – King Midas' castle

DAUGHTER: *Oh father, I am so sad.*

MIDAS: *No, my dear daughter. Why are you sad?*

DAUGHTER: *'Cause I feel so lonely surrounded by all this gold and I cannot enjoy things.*

NARRATOR: *The king was moved by his daughter sorrow and hugged her. When he did it, she was turned into gold.*

MIDAS: *No! What have I done? My precious daughter!*

NARRATOR: *Horrified with what had happened, Midas went looking for the god.*

Scene 3 – Wizard's cottage

MIDAS: *Please, kind god! **Take back** my wish! My daughter is worth more than gold to me!*

WIZARD: *I **warned** you, Midas. I can't undo the gift I granted you. You can try to go to the most dangerous river of the land and get into its water. If you are brave enough, you are free of the spell.*

NARRATOR: *And so Midas did it. Fighting bravely for his life.*

GLOSSARY

Acknowledgment: reconhecimento.

Came out of (to come out of): saiu de (sair de).

Endure (to endure): suportar.

Grant (to grant): conceder.

Take back (to take back): pegar de volta.

Warned (to warn): avisou (avisar).

111

Theater

Scene 4 – River

MIDAS: I have to do this. My daughter needs me! I must **endure** this for a while.

NARRATOR: *After a few minutes, when Midas* **came out of** *the water, he touched some tree branches.*

MIDAS: They are still green and fresh! I am free!

NARRATOR: *From that day on, king Midas lived happily with his daughter. He had learned that love is what makes a person rich, not gold.*

THE END

Based on the ancient Greek Myth.

a) Write **T** (true) or **F** (false).

- ( ) King Midas' story is about true happiness.

- ( ) The story shows that richness is the most important thing in life.

- ( ) King Midas knew the difference between a blessing and a curse very well.

- ( ) The story teaches us that we can't be slaves of our own desires.

b) Why was King Midas greedy?

_____

_____

c) What did he ask his wizard?

_____

_____

d) What kind of power did he receive? How did he feel at first?

_____

_____

e) What made King Midas change his mind?

_____

f) What lesson did King Midas learn?

_____

2 Pair up with a friend. You are going to change roles as being a king/queen and the god of King Midas's story. Using your notebooks, write three wishes you would ask the god, using First Conditional clauses. First, you will be the one who wishes, and for every wish your classmate will tell if he/she can make it come true. Do not forget to change roles.

3 Analyze the script and answer the questions.

a) What kind of text is it?

_____

b) How are the characters presented?

_____

_____

c) How is the setting shown?

- ( ) It is described in the middle of the lines.

- ( ) It is indicated in between the dialogues.

- ( ) It is described in details before the dialogues.

d) Which of the characters is considered only an omniscient voice? Why?

_____

_____

4 Let's role-play a story. First, write a script to recount the story of your chosen myth, then have fun acting it out. Read the following instructions that will help you to do this task.

> How to Write a Simple Screenplay
>
> * Choose a story to recount.
>
> * List all the characters.
>
> * List all the settings.
>
> * Divide the story into scenes.
>
> * Indicate which characters will be in each scene.
>
> * Write the lines for each scene.
>
> * Be creative.

Tying in

Culture

Brazil – Mythology and Folklore

Myths, legends and folkloric tales are stories, beliefs and customs that have been passed down from one generation to the next and are usually conveyed by word of mouth. […]

Gradually, as South America was colonised and inhabited by other cultures from the 16th century onwards, the folklore and myths became infused with influences from the African slaves, Portuguese settlers, and other European folklore […] There are dozens of well-known figures within the Brazilian folklore. Just some of these are:

Available at: <www.brazil.org.za/mythology-and-folklore.html>. Access: Aug. 2018.

Caipora

Caipora is a fantastic creature of the forest, in the Tupi-Guarani mythology: a giant creature, covered with dark hair, who always rides a large boar.

Cobra-Grande

The most powerful mythical creature of the rivers of the Amazon, also called boiúna or mboiaçu. The cobra-grande (large serpent) lives in the water and can take different shapes to frighten away the fishermen.

Iara

Also known as "mãe-d'água" (mother of the waters). […] In the 19th century, a process of convergence occurred, between the Amazonian water snake and the European myth of the beautiful half-human, half-fish creature who lures fishermen with her song.

Salamanca do Jarau

A legend of southern Brazil, the Salamanca is a cave full of treasures, looked after by a magical lizard called teiniaguá.

Available at: <www.maria-brazil.org/brazilian_myths_and_fantastic_creatures.htm>.
Access: Aug. 2018.

GLOSSARY

Boar: javali.
Conveyed (to convey): transmitido (transmitir).
Dozens: dezenas.
Lizard: lagarto.
Onwards: em diante.

Let's practice

1) What are folkloric stories?
_____
_____
_____

2) What happened to South American myths from the 16th century onwards?
_____
_____
_____

3) Which Brazilian mythological figures are mentioned in the text?
_____
_____
_____

4) Match the mythological figure and its definition.

Caipora • Iara • Salamanca do Jarau • Cobra-Grande

a) It looks after a cave of treasures. _____

b) It is a half-human, half-fish creature. _____

c) It is a large serpent that lives in the rivers. _____

d) It is covered with dark hair and it rides a boar. _____

PROJECT

World's best known Mythological Figures

Divide the class into eight groups. Each group will research the mythological figures of one of the following places: North America, Central America, South America, Africa, Asia, Europe, Middle East, and Oceania.
Make an explanative chart and present it to your classmates.

▶II EXPLORING

- *Jack, the Giant Slayer*, 2013.
- *PomPoko*, 1994.
- *Song of the Sea*, 2014.

UNIT 8: WHAT IF WE TOOK BETTER CARE OF NATURE?

||| Get ready |||

1 **What kinds of text do the images represent?**

- ◯ Products ads.
- ◯ Attraction flyers.
- ◯ Campaign pamphlets.
- ◯ Posters.
- ◯ News.
- ◯ Graffiti.

2 **What kind of content do they show?**

- ◯ Shopping promotions.
- ◯ Environmental issues.
- ◯ Worldwide news.
- ◯ Population education.
- ◯ International politics.
- ◯ Different cultures.

3 **Environmental campaigns are everywhere. Do you usually pay attention to their messages? What do you observe?**

_____

_____

_____

117

Let's practice

1) Read the following questions and answer them in groups.

a) What industrialized products do you buy and cannot live without? Why?

b) Can you imagine life without ordinary itens like plastic packages, electricity, cars, etc? How would it be?

c) What would happen if there were no more raw materials to produce new things?

d) What is the importance of renewable and non-renewable materials?

e) What is the objective of recycling? What is its positive impact on the environment?

2) Which of these products can be recycled and which of them cannot? Exchange ideas with a partner and complete the table. Add other materials.

plastic bottle • batteries • lamp bulbs • newspaper

Recyclable	Non-recyclable

3) Organize the activities below into the correct category and find out five ways of going greener and five actions to quit doing.

Use reusable bags.
Use paper napkins.
Use cloth napkins instead of paper ones.
Leave leaks unfixed.
Use plastic bags.
Reuse scrap paper.
Use new sheets of paper.
Fix leaky faucets.
Use no reusable containers.
Repurpose glass jars as leftover containers.

Go greener	Avoid

4 In groups of four, play this Recycling Board Game.

HEADS - Move 2 spaces   TAILS - Move 1 space

Let's listen n' speak

1 Listen to Kevin and Ann talking about the World Environment Day.

a) What is the central idea of having a World Environment Day?
_____
_____

b) When did it start? Who established it?
_____

c) What activities can people do during the week of June 5th?
_____
_____

d) What countries are part of the World Environment Day?
_____

e) Where is June 5th celebrated every year?
_____
_____

f) "The main colors featured in many promotions for this event are natural colors depicting nature, the Earth, and its natural resources". Which colors are these?
_____

g) The campaigns to support the day are promoted by the images of:
_____

2 Pair up and interview a classmate.

- Do you know what renewable and non-renewable materials are? Where do we use them?
- How do you cooperate with the environment? Give examples.
- Would you like Brazil to take part of World Environment Day?
- What other campaigns could be held to support and protect the environment?

CHAPTER 2

Let's practice

1 Match the columns to form sentences in the second conditional.

a) If he started his homework sooner,

b) If you worked harder,

c) If you wanted to feel rested tomorrow,

d) If I were you,

e) If she flew to Canada,

- ( ) she might visit her sister.
- ( ) you could go to be early.
- ( ) I wouldn't disobey the teacher.
- ( ) he would finish it in time.
- ( ) you would do well on the test.

2 Complete the sentences with the correct form of the verbs in the Second Conditional.

a) If we _____ a yacht, we _____ around the world. (to have; to sail)

b) If he_____ more time, he _____ to speak Japanese. (to have; to learn)

c) If they _____ their father about taking the car without his permission, he _____ (be) very angry. (to tell; to be)

d) She _____ a year in the USA if it _____ easier to get a student visa. (to spend; to be)

> **LANGUAGE PIECE**
>
> **Second conditional**
>
> **If** + **subject pronoun** + **main verb** (**simple past**) + complement, + **subject pronoun** + **auxiliary verb** (**would / might**) + **main verb** (**infinitive**) + complement.
>
> **If you studied, you would/ might learn** English faster.

3 Choose the best alternative to complete the sentences.

a) I would help her if she _____ me.
- ( ) will ask
- ( ) asked
- ( ) asks

b) If I were hungry, I _____ a sandwich.
- ( ) make
- ( ) will make
- ( ) would make

c) I would buy a new car if I _____ more money.
- ( ) had
- ( ) have
- ( ) will have

d) If our parents were here, they _____ us what to do.
- ( ) told
- ( ) could tell
- ( ) tell

4 **Unscramble the words to write sentences in the third conditional.**

a) have / told / me / would / if / remembered / I / you'd / the / story /it

_____

_____

b) would / had / have / studied / more / passed / the / exam / she / if / Mary

_____

_____

c) the / train / if / we / have / hadn't / missed / we / would / arrived / on / time

_____

> **LANGUAGE PIECE**
>
> **Third conditional**
>
> **If** + **subject pronoun** + **auxiliary verb** (**had**) + **main verb** (**past perfect**) + complement,
>
> + **subject pronoun** + **auxiliary verb** (**would / could**) + **auxiliary verb** (**have**) + **main verb** (**past perfect**) + complement
>
> **If you had studied, you would/could have passed** the final exam.
>
> If you hadn't called, I would not (wouldn't) have remembered about the test.

_____

d) If / been / there / have / met / the / singer / you / had / could / you

_____

e) I / If / could / have / I'd / in / trouble / known / you / helped / were

_____

f) have / told / me / would / If / remembered / I / you'd / it

_____

g) would / had / have / revised / more / passed / the exam / she / If / she

_____

5 **Circle the correct modal verb to complete each sentence.**

a) There is a good chance that we (might / could) have to postpone the meeting.

b) The volleyball team (can / could) go to the Olympics this year if they are lucky.

c) The airplane has a broken engine, it (might / may) crash.

d) I (could / might) help you with your homework now.

e) There is a small chance the we (could / might) go to the beach this weekend.

f) Five years ago, I (might not / couldn't) play the piano.

Let's listen n' speak

1 Listen to the conversation and answer the questions.

a) Why is Marty upset?
_____

b) Who is responsible for Global Warming, according to Marty?
_____

c) How have humans been harming the environment?
_____

d) Do Bob and Martin think they can do something about the problem? If so, what could they do to help solve this problem?
_____
_____

2 Listen again and complete the sentences.

a) The planet _____ have been in danger if we _____ more careful.

b) If we _____ use so much plastic, the oceans _____ so polluted and the animals _____ because they eat plastic!

c) We _____ stop using plastic straws, for example, or we _____ use reusable bags instead of plastic shopping bags.

d) We _____ also talk about it with friends and family so that they also start changing their habits.

3 Pairs work: follow the instructions.

a) Discuss what you can do in your community and write your ideas on your notebook.

b) Use the list you came up with to make sentences with **could** or **might**. Use your notebook to take notes.

c) Now, on your notebook, write a summary of the ideas you discussed using sentences in the third conditional.

123

Let's practice

1 Choose the words to complete each sentence.

a) _____ help him with the ecofriendly campaign, would you help?
(he / to / if / would / asked / asks / you)

b) Would you be so environmental concerned _____?
(to / weren't / there / problems / if / did / resources)

c) _____ containers if there were more options?
(consume / you / left / less / plastic / if / would)

d) If she _____, _____
helping her out with the campaign.
(he / conscious / wouldn't / isn't / weren't / being / be)

e) If people _____, _____
be more renewable resources.
(more / would / there / prudent / wouldn't / were / are)

2 Write if the following sentences are in **SC** (second conditional) or **TC** (third conditional).

a) ( ) If the students hadn't been late for the exam, they would have passed.

b) ( ) If the weather hadn't been so cold, we would have gone to the beach.

c) ( ) If she had her laptop with her, she would email me.

d) ( ) If the baby had slept better last night, I wouldn't have been so tired.

e) ( ) If Lucy had enough time, she would travel more.

f) ( ) If I wanted a new car, I would buy one.

g) ( ) If José didn't speak good French, he wouldn't move to Paris.

LANGUAGE PIECE

Intonation

Note the intonation in conditional sentences. The if-clause has rising intonation and the dependent clause has falling intonation.

This helps the listener to understand you better.

Let's read n' write

1. Read the following article about natural resources and answer the questions.

What happens when the world's resources run out?

Signs **loom** that we are **nearing** a **crossroads**: demand for the stuff that fuels modern life is **outpacing supply**. Things could get ugly, fast.

BY JOEL HILLIKER • April 11, 2012

The complex modern way of life that has **increasingly besieged** the planet in recent generations is **devouring** resources far faster than ever in human history. Not just obvious things like oil, coal and natural gas, but also a **host of metals**, minerals and elements that we use every day.

If industrialized nations started running out of some of these things, massive **disruptions** would result. [...] History is full of examples, both human and **otherwise**, of the **chilling** consequences to a society or population that **overruns** its resources.[...]

William Rees and Mathis Wackernagel have produced a model for estimating the ecological demands that various **standards** of living put on the planet, called the Global Footprint Network (GFN). They estimate that the **average person on Earth** needs 4.4 acres of land and sea to support him. Considering living standards, the average person in China needs 5.4 **acres**, while the typical American needs nearly 20 acres.

This model has produced the same conclusion that several other sources have, including the United Nations: that for all people to have a standard of living like the average American would take four or five more Earths' worth of resources.

The reality is, **current** demand is *already* rapidly **depleting** supplies of finite resources such as oil, coal, natural gas, metals, minerals and even water. New discoveries of easily accessed sources are getting more rare, and older sources are declining in **output**. [...]

Joel Hilliker, The trumpet.com. Available at: <www.thetrumpet.com/article/9302.8138.0.0/world/what-happens-when-the-worlds-resources-run-out>. Access: Oct. 2018.

GLOSSARY

Acres: acre (unidade de medida de área equivalente a 4.042m).
Chilling: terrível.
Crossroads: encruzilhada.
Current: atual.
Depleting (to deplete): esgotando (esgotar).
Devouring (to devour): devorando (devorar).
Disruptions: interrupções.
Host of metals: uma variedade de metais.
Increasingly besieged: aumentado o assédio.
Loom (to loom): aparecem, assomam (aparecer, assomar).
Nearing (to near): aproximando (aproximar).
Otherwise: de outra forma.
Outpacing supply (to outpace supply): superando os recursos (superar os recursos).
Output: produção.
Overruns (to overrun): excede (exceder).
Run out (to run out): acabar, esgotar.
Standards: padrões.

a) What is the concern presented in the text?

_____

_____

b) Why does modern life demand so much? What are the consequences of this demand?

_____

_____

_____

c) What does _"Considering living standards, the average person in China needs 5.4 acres, while the typical American needs nearly 20 acres"_ mean?

_____

_____

_____

d) How many Earth's worth resources would be necessary for all people to have an average American standard of living?

_____

e) Which finite resources are mentioned in the text?

_____

f) Read the question below and discuss with your classmates. Write down your ideas about it. Use conditional sentences.

> What happens when the world's resources run out?

_____

_____

_____

_____

_____

2 Analyze the newspaper article and answer the questions.

a) What kind of text is it?

_____

b) What is the aim of the text?

_____

c) What kind of language is used in it?

_____

d) What elements are part of this type of text?

_____

_____

e) What kind of text is an article? What information does it bring? Check all that apply.

- ( ) Empirical facts.
- ( ) Data.
- ( ) Descriptive.

- ( ) Informative.
- ( ) Hypothesis.
- ( ) Persuasive.

f) Where can texts like this be found?

_____

3 Let's write a news article regarding the future of world's natural resources. Read the tips below to help you out.

* Research the world's renewable and non-renewable resources.

* Gather data in reliable sources and by trustworthy authorities.

* Select images that illustrate the information you gather.

* Write a draft and make a peer evaluation of it with your classmates.

* Write a new version of the article, making all the necessary adjustments.

* Hand it in to your teacher.

||| Citizenship moment |||
///// REDUCE /// REUSE /// RECYCLE /////

NATURAL RESOURCES

Natural resources are those elements of the environment that are considered valuable to humans. These can be raw materials, such as trees for lumber and ore for manufacturing, or things that are directly consumed, such as groundwater to drink and animals to eat.

RENEWABLE RESOURCES
They are the resources that are not in danger of being used up, it means they can be replenished or reproduced easily, like sunlight, air, trees, crops, etc.

NON-RENEWABLE RESOURCES
They are found in fixed amounts once they are formed over very long geological periods. These resources are essentially finite, and cannot be replaced. They are found inside the earth, like fossil fuels, mineral resources, coal, natural gas, etc.

⚠ NATURAL RESOURCES OVERRUN ⚠

Humans have been irresponsibly using the natural resources without considering the consequences it can have upon humanity. Many of the non-renewable resources known are in danger of being extinguished. The demand for these resources are outpacing their capability of supply.
People need to reset the way of consuming in order to avoid bigger problems in a near future, such as applying the 3 R's in the daily life.

THE 3 R'S OF THE ENVIRONMENT

Don't buy things you don't need or items that come in wasteful packaging or that cannot be recycled. Reuse and recycle whatever you can.

REDUCE
Reducing the amount of waste you produce by choosing what rubbish to throw away:
- Make slight alterations in the shopping list: buy only what is needed, buy products that can be reused and with little packaging, sell or give away unwanted items, and reduce paper waste;
- Deal with hazardous products in the correct manner, buy non-toxic products or find safer alternatives;
- Think of the possible uses things can have before throwing them away.

REUSE
Instead of throwing things away, try to find ways to use them again, like:
- Donate old electrical equipment, clothes, and books;
- Make a car-boot sale with unwanted items;
- Build a compost bin.

RECYCLE
Create new products out of the materials from the old ones by:
- Finding ways of recycling different materials;
- Buying products that can be recycled or that are made out of recycled materials;
- Avoiding buying hazardous materials;
- Using recycle bins.

GLOSSARY

Bin: lixeira.
Car-boot sale: forma de mercado em que as pessoas se reúnem para vender produtos domésticos e artigos de jardinagem que são colocados no porta--malas (boot) dos automóveis.
Compost bin: depósito de compostagem.
Crops: safra.
Finite: limitado.
Fossil fuels: combustíveis fósseis.
Geological: geológico.
Groundwater: água subterrânea.
Hazardous: perigoso.
Lumber: tábuas de madeira.
Manner: maneira.
Ore: minério.
Packaging: embalagem.
Raw material: matéria--prima.
Replenished (to replenish)): reabastecido (reabastecer).
Reproduced (to reproduce): reproduzido (reproduzir).
Reset (to reset): reestabelecer, recompor.
Resource: fonte, recurso.
Rubbish: lixo.
Valuable: valioso.
Wasteful: que causa desperdício.

Based on: <https://kids.niehs.nih.gov/topics/reduce/index.htm>; <https://kids.niehs.nih.gov/topics/reduce/reduce-waste/index.htm>; <https://kids.niehs.nih.gov/topics/reduce/reuse/index.htm>; <https://kids.niehs.nih.gov/topics/reduce/recycle/index.htm>. Access: Sep. 2018.

Let's practice

1) Read the text and answer.

a) What are natural resources? Give examples.

_____

_____

_____

b) What is the difference between renewable and non-renewable resources?

_____

_____

_____

PROJECT

Expressions

Team up with three friends and research to discover more information about the expressions **eco-friendly actions** and **go greener**. Bring your notes to class and share thoughts and findings with the other groups.

2) Explain the meaning of each R presented in the text. Give other examples for each of them.

a) Reduce:

_____

_____

_____

b) Reuse:

_____

_____

c) Recycle:

_____

EXPLORING

Earth Overshoot Day
- www.overshootday.org/

Recycling Guide
- www.recycling-guide.org.uk/rrr.html

EcoKids
- www.ecokidsusa.org/3rs.html

3) Answer with your classmates.

a) Do you use the plastic bags from the stores or do you carry your own shopping bag?

b) Does your community offer a recycling program?

c) Which sounds more important nowadays: to keep the standard of life or to recover and protect the environment?

d) Who is more responsible for pollution and waste: individuals, corporations, or the government?

REVIEW

1) Complete the sentences using the appropriate conditional.

a) If it rains, _____

b) If it rained, _____

c) If it had rained, _____

d) I would buy a new tablet _____

e) I will give you a present _____

f) Our planet wouldn't have been so damaged _____

2) Read the definitions below and check only the ones that explain the meaning of the word 'myth'.

- ◯ A usually traditional story of ostensibly historical events that serves to unfold part of the world view of a people or explain a practice, belief, or natural phenomenon. (Merrian-Webster Dictionary)

- ◯ A traditional story, especially one concerning the early history of a people or explaining some natural or social phenomenon, and typically involving supernatural beings or events. (Oxford Living Dictionaries)

- ◯ A book that someone writes about someone else's life or about their own life. (Macmillan Dictionary)

- ◯ An official document which a group of people issue after investigating a situation or event. (Collins Dictionary)

3) Rewrite the sentences in the third conditional. Make sure to keep the same meaning.

a) She did not give me her phone number. I could not call her.

_____

b) He was at work. He could not go to the movies.

_____

c) We did not have any sugar. I did not make cake.

_____

d) I traveled to five different countries because I won the lottery.

_____

4 **Match the questions to the answers.**

a) What would you do if you could be invisible for a day?

b) What will you do if your brother wears your clothes?

c) What would you have done if your kids had lied to you?

d) What will you do if you have a free day next week?

- ( ) I would have grounded them.

- ( ) I would spy on my friends.

- ( ) I will tell my parents.

- ( ) I will watch some movies.

5 **Circle the mistakes and rewrite the sentences correctly.**

a) If you read this book, I'm sure you had loved it!

_____

b) What will you do if you were invisible?

_____

c) We wouldn't have missed the bus if we had leave home on time.

_____

d) If you wouldn't have a bike, how would you go to school?

_____

6 **Unscramble the words and make correct sentences.**

a) have prepared / I could / dinner / if you had / you were / hungry. / told me.

_____

b) gone by subway / They might have / if they had / the car accident. / known about.

_____

_____

c) saved the money, / If she had / could she have / that car? / bought

_____

_____

DO NOT FORGET!

CONDITIONAL SENTENCES
Statements discussing known factors or hypothetical situations and their consequences.

FIRST CONDITIONAL
Used to express situations in which the consequence or outcome is likely (but not guaranteed) to happen in the future.

EXAMPLES
If you **study**, you **will** pass the examinations.

If you **don't cry**, **I'll** give you a gift.

Will you help me **if I pay** you?

SECOND CONDITIONAL
Used to express outcomes or consequences that are completely unrealistic or will not likely happen in the future.

EXAMPLES
If I **were** you, I **would** study more.

What **would** you do **if** you **could** skip work today?

We **wouldn't** go there if we **didn't need** to.

THIRD CONDITIONAL
Used to explain that present circumstances would be different if something else had happened in the past.

EXAMPLES
What **would** you **have done if** you **had been** there?

If she **had studied** more, she **would have gotten** a better grade.

GO GREENER!

- Use reusable bags.
- Don't use paper napkins.
- Use cloth napkins.
- Don't leave leaks unfixed.
- Don't use plastic bags.
- Reuse scrap paper.
- Don't use new sheets of paper.
- Fix leaky faucets.
- Use reusable containers.
- Repurpose glass jars as leftover containers.
- Prefer recyclable products.
- Recycle.

MYTH

RELATED WORDS OR EXPRESSIONS
- A traditional story.
- Expresses beliefs and values.
- A story about evil and good.
- About gods, sacred, and supernatural creatures.
- Cultural traditions.

MODALS: MIGHT AND COULD

Express degrees of possibility.

I could have helped him if he had asked me.
I might have helped him if he had asked me.

132

OVERCOMING CHALLENGES

(ESPM-SP – 2011)

(November 18, 1985 *Calvin and Hobbes* by Bill Watterson)

Turning the third frame of the strip into the third conditional, we would have:

a) "And if anything had been, by Golly, I would have been ready for it!"

b) "And if anything happened, by Golly, I'd be ready for it!"

c) "And if anything did, by Golly, I would be ready for it!"

d) "And had anything happened, by Golly, I'd have been ready for it!"

e) "And if anything had happened, by Golly, I'd be ready for it!"

(CEUMA)

Complete the sentence correctly: "I _____ that house, if I were you."

a) had son

c) would sell

e) will sell

b) has sold

d) sold

(Mackenzie-SP)

Complete with the correct verb tense.

> **I.** If I _____ it, would visit you.
> **II.** If she is sad, I'll _____ her a story.
> **III.** If you lit the room, we _____ better.
> **IV.** If you _____ angry, don't shout at me.

a) know – tells – will see – is

b) know – told – would see – am

c) knows – tells – would see – is

d) knew – told – is seeing – were

e) knew – tell – would see – are

WORKBOOK

||| Unit 1 |||

1 Match the columns in order to make correct sentences.

a) Kevin will apply… • ( ) … a job.

b) I will graduate… • ( ) … to college at his final year of high school.

c) My friends' plan… • ( ) … is to go abroad in a few months.

d) Allison really needs to get… • ( ) … from college in some years.

2 Rewrite the following sentences in their interrogative and negative forms.

a) Joanne will study law when she grows up.

- Interrogative: _____

- Negative: _____

b) They will get married in a few months.

- Interrogative: _____

- Negative: _____

c) In the future, my country will have better opportunities for the generations to come.

- Interrogative: _____

- Negative: _____

3 Complete the gaps with **so**, **if**, **then** or **because**.

a) I won't go to the party _____ my clothes are not adequate.

b) I was late for class, _____ my teacher didn't let me in.

c) _____ it rains, I won't go to the concert.

d) She will go to school and _____ she will visit Mary at the hospital.

4 What will Erick study when he grows up?

a) Medicine _____

b) Law _____

c) Engineering _____

d) Design _____

5 **Circle the mistakes and rewrite the sentences.**

a) The show was canceled if the singer was not feeling well.

_____

b) My dad cleaned all the house, and because he decided to go to the club.

_____

c) I don't like orange juice, if I will have some water, please.

_____

d) I can't tell then he is telling the truth or not. Let's talk to his parents.

_____

6 **Mia will finish school and then she'll go to college. Write sentences describing what she thinks will happen when she does.**

a) To have painting lessons _____

b) To study chemistry _____

c) To study until late _____

d) To have many new friends _____

e) To find the love of her life _____

7 **Write sentences using the given clues.**

a) I – think – will – to travel – next year – because – to have – the money

_____

b) I – don't think – she – will – to need – to use the car – so – can – to use – it

_____

c) They – probably – will – to study – law – then – become – judges

_____

d) We – definitely – will – to visit – you – if – to go – to NY

_____

WORKBOOK

||| Unit 2 |||

1 **Read the sentences and rewrite them in their negative and interrogative forms.**

a) I am going to sleep here.

- Negative: _____

- Interrogative: _____

b) We are going to apply for college on Wednesday.

- Negative: _____

- Interrogative: _____

c) Doug is going to lend me his car this weekend.

- Negative: _____

- Interrogative: _____

2 **Read the sentences and decide if they are in the PC (present continuous) or FS (future simple) tense.**

a) ◯ Steve is watching TV now.

b) ◯ Alan is going to study in Canada next year.

c) ◯ Amanda is going to school right now.

d) ◯ Allison, are you going to the concert next week?

3 **Give short answers for the questions below.**

a) Is Marina going to buy those clothes?

- Affirmative: _____   • Negative: _____

b) Are you and Sally going to visit me when I arrive?

- Affirmative: _____   • Negative: _____

c) Are the kids going to play at the park?

- Affirmative: _____   • Negative: _____

d) Is Mrs. Gibson going to give you a ride to school?

- Affirmative: _____   • Negative: _____

4 Read Samuel's opinion and answer the questions.

My name is Samuel, I'm 16 and I'm going to vote for the first time this year.
I'm not really sure if I have a candidate who I like. We are going to choose a mayor and a president, and I believe that these are the most important political positions, so I need to vote carefully.

a) What is Samuel going to do for the first time this year?
_____

b) What political positions are going to be voted?
_____

c) Why does Samuel think he needs to vote carefully?
_____

5 Write questions for the following answers.

a) _____
Yes, I am going to save some money for the school trip.

b) _____
No, we aren't going to school tomorrow.

c) _____
Yes, she is going to like the present. It is her favorite kind of book.

d) _____
Yes, it is going to rain tomorrow. I'm sure about that.

6 Write true sentences about your future plans.
_____
_____
_____

WORKBOOK

||| Unit 3 |||

1 How do people move around? Label each option correctly.

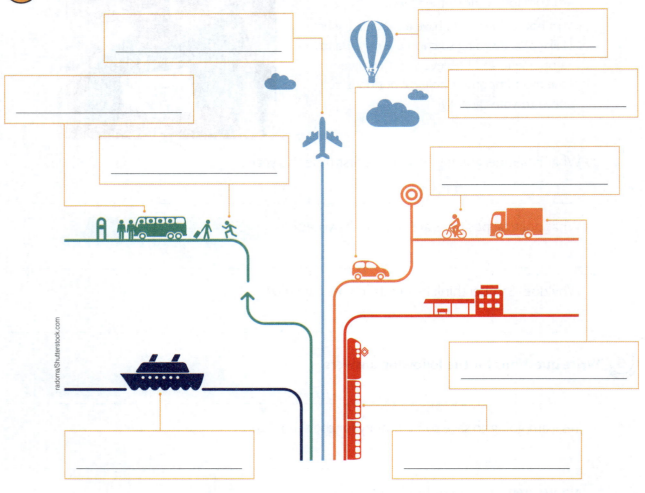

2 Analyze the questions and decide if they are **E** (embedded) or **D** (direct).

a) ◯ How old are you?

b) ◯ What time does the history class start?

c) ◯ Can you tell me what his name is?

d) ◯ Do you know when Mary arrived?

3 Rewrite the questions below in their direct form.

a) Do you know how old he is?

_____

b) Can you tell me where that girl studies?

_____

4 Unscramble the words and form sentences.

a) I probably to the party subway tomorrow will go evening by.

_____

b) vacation We going travel by to ship on our are next!

_____

c) coming He on is foot, he coming by isn't bike.

_____

5 Complete the missing part of the sentences.

a) Tell me, Sarah, what are you _____ to do tomorrow afternoon?

b) _____ Elizabeth cook dinner tonight, if she has the time?

c) The kids _____ going to play outside after school, they are going to study in their bedroom. They are grounded.

d) Bob, _____ your mother going to the mall by car after work?

e) The teachers _____ talk to the student's parents if they come to the meeting.

6 Circle the mistakes and rewrite the sentences.

a) Albert is going buy some fruits at the market this afternoon.

_____

b) Dennis and Steve are will not take their car to the garage tomorrow.

_____

c) Allison, will you going to study for tomorrow's test?

_____

d) Mr. and Mrs. McDouglas are go to buy a new beach house this year.

_____

e) I will to get into college as soon as I finish high school.

_____

WORKBOOK

||| Unit 4 |||

1 Find the eight words related to technology in the word search below.

S	C	O	M	P	U	T	E	R	B	T
T	C	D	E	F	G	H	M	I	J	Y
R	K	L	M	N	O	P	A	Q	R	P
E	S	T	W	E	E	T	I	N	G	W
A	T	U	V	X	Z	K	L	W	Y	R
M	Z	K	W	Y	A	E	I	O	U	I
I	B	D	C	F	G	H	L	J	K	T
N	G	R	A	M	O	P	H	O	N	E
G	M	T	E	X	T	I	N	G	X	R
Y	S	M	A	R	T	P	H	O	N	E

2 Choose the best option to complete the sentences.

a) Edward is really sick. He _____ go to the doctor soon, before he gets even worse. (had better / ought to)

b) In my opinion, you _____ wear the pink dress for the party. It's very beautiful and fancy. (should / had better)

c) Mr. Brown, you _____ read this report if you want to understand this company's policy. (ought to / had better)

d) Zach, you _____ tell your parents the truth before they find it out, or you'll be in trouble. (ought to / had better)

3 Rewrite the sentences replacing the underlined modal verbs with others with the same meaning.

a) You <u>must</u> do everything he says.

_____

b) In this school, all students <u>need to</u> wear uniforms.

_____

c) All my friends <u>should</u> be invited to my birthday party!

_____

4 **Read the following sentences and answer the questions.**

a) You should use social networking sites carefully.

b) You must never give your personal information to people you meet in chat rooms.

c) You have to have internet access to go online.

d) You need to have a computer, tablet, or smartphone if you want to use instant messaging apps.

e) Kids and teens ought to be careful when texting other people.

f) I think kids and teens had better ask their parents' permission before visiting any website.

g) Teachers should inform their students about the dangers and benefits of posting on forums.

- Which sentences express an advice or suggestion? _____

- Which modal verbs were used in these sentences? _____

- Which sentences express an obligation or a necessity? _____

- Which modal verbs were used in these sentences?

  _____

- Write an advice regarding internet technology usage. Use the modal verbs.

  _____

- Write a sentence expressing obligation or necessity regarding internet technology usage. Use the modal verbs.

  _____

5 **Write sentences using the given information.**

a) You – have to – to use the tablet (negative)

_____

b) I – need to – to post on the blog (interrogative)

_____

c) The kids – ought to – to try this new ice cream flavor (affirmative)

_____

d) Jack – must – to obey his parents (affirmative)

_____

WORKBOOK

||| Unit 5 |||

1) Choose the correct sentence.

a) ◯ Nuria had listen to Jonas Brothers before she played hopscotch.
   ◯ Nuria had listened to Jonas Brothers before she played hopscotch.

b) ◯ We had not started Aqua Play when the popcorn was ready.
   ◯ We had started not Aqua Play when the popcorn was ready.

c) ◯ When Gal drew Phineas and Ferb, she had eaten her dinner.
   ◯ When Gal drew Phineas and Ferb, she has eaten her dinner.

2) Write questions about Pat's weekly schedule.

	Monday	Tuesday	Wednesday	Thursday	Friday
morning	play Wii		watch Dora and Diego		
afternoon			have Chinese jump rope championship		read Harry Potter book
evening				have a milkshake	go bowling

_____

_____

_____

3) Now, answer the questions you wrote in the previous exercise.

_____

_____

_____

_____

4 **Write sentences according to the given order.**

a) 1 – We got home; 2 – We watched a movie

_____

b) 2 – Derek had a headache; 1 – He played in the sun for 2 hours

_____

c) 2 – Val met me at the mall; 1. We called each other

_____

d) 1 – My parents argued; 2 – They went separate ways

_____

e) 2 – We stopped to have lunch; 1 – We drove for hours

_____

5 **Match the columns.**

a) By the time I cleared the table

b) Did they cut your phone line again?

c) If you had come earlier,

d) They had not looked at the map,

e) I know you want all those books,

- ( ) I thought the problem had been solved.

- ( ) we would have had more time to talk about this.

- ( ) but we had talked about saving before coming here right?

- ( ) had you finished eating?

- ( ) so they got lost.

6 **Complete the gaps with the simple past or past perfect form of the verbs.**

a) Ferdinand _____ his homework before he _____ skating. (to do / to begin)

b) We _____ to the parents before they _____ to take their son to another school. (to talk / to decide)

c) Before the kids _____ the window, they _____ their bicycle. (to break / to break)

d) Ingrid _____ popcorn when she _____ play to watch the movie. (to make / to press)

WORKBOOK

||| Unit 6 |||

1) Complete the sentences with your own ideas.

a) The pyramids _____

b) Printers _____

c) Every year _____

d) Apps _____

e) Paper _____

2) Decide if the sentence is C (correct) or I (incorrect). Circle the mistakes and rewrite the incorrect ones.

a) ◯ Taj Mahal is finished in 1652.

b) ◯ 388 thousand tons of napalm was dropped in Vietnam, from 1963 to 1973.

c) ◯ iPod was launched in 2001.

d) ◯ In Angra 1,640 MW of energy are produced every year.

e) ◯ Some bacteria and fungi are use to clean rivers in São Paulo.

_____

_____

_____

3) Rewrite the sentences in the passive voice.

a) The kids do the washing up.

_____

b) Sensors control the door.

_____

c) IBM CPU stored 160 KB (past).

_____

d) NASA paid Neil Armstrong U$20,000 to go to the Moon (past).

_____

4 Complete the text with the passive form of the verbs.

ICAN

Nuclear weapons are the most destructive, inhumane and indiscriminate weapons ever created. Both in the scale of the devastation they cause, and in their uniquely persistent, spreading, genetically damaging radioactive fallout, they are unlike any other weapons. A single nuclear bomb that

_____ (to detonate) over a large city could kill millions of people. The use of tens or hundreds of nuclear bombs would disrupt the global climate, causing widespread famine.

ICAN _____ a coalition _____ (to form) of several hundred non-government organizations, from local peace groups to global federations representing millions of people. An international steering group and staff team coordinate the campaign's activities. Our main

office _____ (to locate) in Geneva, Switzerland.

Available at: <http://www.icanw.org/the-facts/catastrophic-harm/>. Access: Sep. 2018.

5 Choose the correct options to complete each sentence.

a) Who _____?
- ◯ was this invented.
- ◯ was this invention.
- ◯ was this invented by.

b) We _____ last night.
- ◯ destroyed the house
- ◯ were destroyed the house
- ◯ are destroyed

c) How often _____ cables _____?
- ◯ do / checked
- ◯ are / fixed
- ◯ are / checked

d) When we are young, we _____ what to do a million times.
- ◯ are told
- ◯ are telling
- ◯ is told

145

WORKBOOK

||| Unit 7 |||

1) Match the columns to form sentences.

a) If you study for the math text,
b) Alicia will get really mad
c) We will see a doctor
d) If I get that raise,

- ( ) if you don't get better soon.
- ( ) I'm sure you will get an A.
- ( ) if she discovers you lied to her.
- ( ) we'll get you a new car.

2) Unscramble the words and write correct sentences.

a) the party Elliot invite will to if come you him.
_____

b) need help, just If you tell my me!
_____

c) get sick that if continues She will eating all junk she food.
_____
_____

d) they If they the time have, will the museum visit.
_____
_____

3) Rewrite the underlined parts of the sentences in their negative forms.

a) <u>If you come</u>, I'll be sad.
_____

b) <u>He will have the money</u> if he buys that house.
_____

c) <u>She will accept it</u> if you talk to her.
_____

d) If you leave, <u>call me back</u>.
_____

4 Complete the missing words to make conditional sentences.

a) What _____ you do _____ he calls you?

b) _____ they arrive here late, _____ they miss their flight?

c) Where _____ he stay _____ he decides to come along?

d) _____ you accept it _____ she apologizes?

e) _____ you get upset _____ they play with your things?

5 Complete the dialogue with the words from the box.

> mythological · gods · if · myths · will · box · mortal

Barry: I really like _____. And you, Cindy?

Cindy: Me too. My favorite one is about Pandora and her _____. I think it's really interesting.

Barry: I like that one, too. Listen, my favorite _____ figure is Hercules.
Cindy: Hercules? Why?
Barry: He was the son of the _____ Zeus and Alcmene. He had god-

like strength, but he was _____.
Cindy: Interesting. I have a book about myths somewhere at home. Maybe one day we could check it together.

Barry: Yeah, maybe. But I prefer movies! _____ you are free this weekend,

_____ you watch a movie about myths with me? It's about Thor, the god of thunder.
Cindy: Sure!

6 Choose the best answer for the questions.

a) What are Barry and Cindy talking about?

- ( ) Biographies.
- ( ) Myths.
- ( ) Documentaries.

b) What is Cindy's favorite Myth?

- ( ) Pandora's box.
- ( ) Hercules.
- ( ) Thor.

c) What does Cindy say she has at home?

- ( ) A book.
- ( ) A movie.
- ( ) A myth.

Unit 8

1. Classify the following items into R (recyclable) or NR (non-recyclable).

a) ( ) newspaper
b) ( ) plastic bottles
c) ( ) lamp bulbs
d) ( ) cardboard paper
e) ( ) batteries
f) ( ) nylon
g) ( ) styrofoam
h) ( ) aluminum cans

2. Circle the right option.

a) If you had told me about your problem, I (can / could) have helped you.
b) If he had studied, he (might / will) have passed the examination.
c) If I were you, I (will / would) ask her out.
d) He would enjoy it if you (invite / invited) him to the party.
e) They would have allowed their son to go to the party if he (had / would) asked them.
f) If it rains, we (will / would) be able to see a beautiful rainbow.

3. What would Peter do if he won the lottery? Use the clues to write sentences using the second conditional.

a) To buy modern furniture

_____

b) To move to a bigger house

_____

c) To go sailing on his own boat

_____

d) To go shopping

_____

e) To travel to a desert island

_____

f) To buy more books

_____

4 Analyze the infographic below and complete the sentences about what we could have done differently in the past to have avoided global warming.

a) If we _____ trash, we _____ caused global warming. (to recycle)

b) If we _____ pollution, we _____ caused global warming. (to avoid)

c) If we _____ fewer trees, we _____ caused global warming. (to cut)

d) If we _____ alternative means of transportation, we _____ caused global warming. (to use)

e) If we _____ our rivers clean, we _____ caused global warming. (to keep)

5 Rewrite the following sentences, replacing the modal verb could for the modal verb might.

a) They could have saved some money if they had stayed at a cheaper hotel.

_____

b) If I had known the test would be so hard, I could have studied more.

_____

c) Mia could have reused the scrap paper if she had learned about recycling.

_____

149

EXPERT'S POINT I

Exchange program

A Year Abroad

You have probably felt the urge to do something different. To chart your own path. Life isn't only about what you see and do in your own country, hometown or school, or even with your friends. What is beyond? You need to challenge yourself, to take a chance. For a school year (or even for a few weeks) you can dare to be different!

What makes an exchange student different? When someone leaves the familiar behind and **plunges into** the unknown, he or she is showing a commitment to understanding other people, to learning about the world in a way that **textbooks** and school assignments never reveal. A year spent abroad is a year that will redefine your world.

You'll discover that every moment, every conversation and experience, challenges the way you look at the world. You'll see differences as well as similarities in people and their actions, in their beliefs and values. You'll experience the **intricately** structured social code of the Japanese, or the **egalitarian** beliefs of the Scandinavians, considered the most socially progressive Europeans. Suddenly you'll realize what it means to belong to a certain country and culture. You'll learn about yourself as you learn about others.

Becoming an exchange student gives you more than knowledge about another country and its language and culture. A year abroad teaches you about building friendships, taking responsibility for yourself, respecting differences and tolerating the beliefs of others.

Exchange students develop leadership skills, self-confidence and a greater understanding of the complexities of the world around them. This is why the best universities, as well as corporations and professionals, look favorably on students who have spent a school year abroad. They know that former international exchange students bring a higher level of maturity and a global frame of reference to their university studies and activities. […]

While you live the typical daily life of another culture, you are learning every minute of every day. You might live in a French city meant for walking, with **cobblestone** streets so narrow you can touch the walls of buildings with **outstretched** arms on both sides. Or you may live in a Spanish village where the remains of an entire castle lie. Perhaps you'll find yourself in Sweden living in a **walled** city dating back to medieval days, or that your **homestay** town in Germany includes a "living castle," an actual private residence still being used today. These are the sorts of discoveries you will make as you learn **firsthand** about what you have only studied in the classroom until now.

You'll also find that the school systems are among the best in the world, and that the teenagers are much the same as they are at home. They work hard at their studies, play sports, love parties and cinema, and pursue hobbies just like you. A few will become your friends for life.

The best way to truly become involved in the culture of a foreign country is to live among its people as a member of a family. […] Host families feel they benefit from the experience as much as you do! They want to learn about your culture and introduce you to theirs. […]

In fact, you'll probably find that after a few weeks you'll be asking them to speak in their native tongue.

This may be hard for you to believe. You might be **wondering** how you'll express yourself; how you'll communicate with store **clerks**, teachers, classmates and your host family. Even if you've studied a foreign language in school, you won't feel ready to live in that language. But when you're surrounded by that language from morning till night, you learn the fastest way possible. It's like a month of classes in a single day! […]

With […] the constant exposure you'll have to the language, you'll be talking comfortably with your host family in just a few weeks. Within four months, exchange students should speak the host country language fluently. You'll tell jokes and **gossip** with friends, even dream and speak to pets in the foreign language. And the fluency you develop will give you a great advantage in your future **schooling** and career.

ASSE

ASSE was established in 1976 to organize student exchange programs. In 1988, it founded EurAupair Intercultural Child Care Programs, and at the turn of the millennium, it founded Aspire Worldwide Work and Travel, Trainee and Intern Programs for university students, graduates, and professionals. In 2009, ASSE and its affiliates founded Go Campus University Programs. ASSE's mission is to foster international understanding through educational and cross-cultural programs.

Available at: <https://asse.com/become_an_asse_exchange_student/student_exchange_program/>. Access: Aug. 2018.

GLOSSARY

Clerks: balconista.

Cobblestone: paralelepípedo.

Egalitarian: igualitário(a).

Firsthand: em primeira mão.

Gossip (to gossip): fofocar.

Homestay: casa de família.

Hometown: cidade natal.

Host (to host): hospedar.

Intricately: intricadamente.

Outstretched: esticado.

Path: caminho.

Plunges into (to plunge into): mergulha em (mergulhar em).

Schooling: escolaridade, aprendizagem.

Textbooks: livros didáticos.

To chart: mapear.

Walled: murado(a).

Wondering (to wonder): imaginando (imaginar).

PROJECT

How to get ready to study abroad

Organized in small groups, discuss the requirements someone should have and what a person should look for to apply for an exchange program. Make a list and research the information needed. Prepare a presentation for your classmates.

EXPERT'S POINT 11

Home and garden

Your guide to green holidays

Although they're full of **merriment**, the holidays can also be a time of unnecessary excess. This time of year should be about family, friends, food and fun — not stuff!

Between late November and early January, **household** waste increases by more than 25 per cent, from extra food waste (up to 40 per cent of festive food is wasted), packaging and trashed old items replaced with newer versions received as gifts. According to the U.S. Environmental Protection Agency, the result is more than one million more tons per week in **landfills** across North America.

Research from the Center for Global Development estimates that holiday lights use 6.6 billion kilowatt hours of electricity per year. Increased travel **boosts** greenhouse gas emissions that contribute to climate change.

The holiday **frenzy** can also cause stress and anxiety. This is where mindfulness comes in!

Here are some tips to maximize your holiday cheer while minimizing environmental impact.

Gifts

- **Shop local** Reduce your **footprint** and support the local economy.
- **Get creative** Instead of buying things, give experiences […]!
- **Buy quality** If you're going to buy, choose what will last. Avoid non-recyclable plastics. Look for ethically made products. […]
- **Do it yourself** Take advantage of your time off! **Knit**, draw, **bake** — put your love into homemade gifts.
- **Donate** Support causes your loved ones care about most, in their honor. […].
- **Don't rush** Choosing rush delivery often means that cargo planes and trucks go out half-empty. […]
- **Recycle: Regifting** is OK – just give your regifted item to someone who'll appreciate it. If you get new tech gadgets, donate or properly recycle your old items.

Wrap

- Erase single-use wrapping and **unleash** creativity! […] Avoid plastic **ribbons**, **bows** and glitter.

Cards

- Choose e-cards to save paper and postage. Personalize them by adding pictures, music and graphics. […]

Food

- **Ditch tinfoil** and plastic. Opt for reusable **beeswax** food wrap, stainless steel or glassware for leftovers.
- Choose local, seasonal vegetables. Hit up farmers markets, organic stores, co-ops and your own garden.
- If you can, eliminate meat. If you're eating meat, eat less and buy what's local and ethically raised.
- Avoid disposables. If you don't have enough reusable items, have guests bring their own!
- Turn down the heat before people arrive. […]

kuppa_rock/iStockphoto.com

Trees
- Opt for potted trees that can be replanted outside. If you want a cut tree, buy from a local, organic tree farm. [...]
- Avoid fake trees. [...]

Lights
- Choose LED lights. They have a longer **life span** and use less energy [...]
- Properly recycle old incandescent lights. [...]

Travel

- If family lives across distances, reduce travel miles by choosing a central location to come together.
- If you must travel by air, buy **carbon offsets**.

The best of the holidays comes from the wealth we create through relationships — to ourselves, to each other and to nature!

Happy holidays!

Expert's profile

David Takayoshi Suzuki

David Takayoshi Suzuki is a geneticist, a broadcaster, and an environmental activist. He is known for his career as a broadcaster as well as his work as an environmental activist to reverse global climate change. He co-founded the David Suzuki Foundation in 1990, which priorities are: oceans and sustainable fishing, climate change and clean energy, sustainability, and Suzuki's Nature Challenge.

Available at: <https://davidsuzuki.org/queen-of-green/your-guide-green-holidays/>. Access: Aug. 2018.

GLOSSARY

Bake (to bake): asse (assar).
Beeswax: cera de abelha.
Boosts (to boost): aumenta (aumentar).
Bows: laços.
Carbon offsets: compensação de carbono.
Tinfoil: papel alumínio.
Footprint: pegada.
Frenzy: frenesi.
Household: casa.
Knit (to knit): tricote (tricotar).
Landfills: aterros sanitários.
Life span: vida útil.
Merriment: alegria.
Ribbons: fitas.
Unleash (to unleash): solte (soltar).

PROJECT

How to make our community eco-friendlier?

Team up and discuss with your friends what other actions you can take to make your community eco-friendlier. Research information that support your ideas and make a poster to present it.

FOCUS ON CULTURE 1

INTERNET SAFETY

Let's face it: Internet is dangerous! But we can be safe with simple actions!

DO NOT HIDE INFORMATION FROM YOUR FAMILY

Nearly **32**% of teenagers delete or hide their browsing history from their parents, allowing cyber-attacks.

DO NOT SHARE EXPLICIT PHOTOS

Researches indicate that one in four teenagers has shared a nude or semi-nude photograph of themselves via the internet. It is important to note that once something crosses the internet, there is no way to remove it.

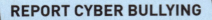

REPORT CYBER BULLYING

Adults, especially senior citizens, are susceptible to cyber bullying, just as are children and teenagers. It is important to never respond to threatening or obscure messages, to always remain diligent and to report any abuse, whether suspected or proven.

BE CAREFUL WITH YOUR PERSONAL INFORMATION

Users under the age of 18 are 51 times more likely to have their identities stolen. Criminals target children because they have clean credit records and frequently post personal information publicly.

Christiane S. Messias

BE RESPONSIBLE WHEN SURFING THE WEB

Visiting insecure or inappropriate websites can compromise your personal and financial information or harm your computer. Security and anti-virus software are a must for all computers.

PEOPLE USING THE INTERNET WORLDWIDE BY AGE IN 2018

- 2-10: 80%
- 11-17: 88%
- 18-29: 88%
- 30-49: 87%
- 50+: 77%

90% Start using the internet before they are 10 years old

KIDS FROM 2 TO 16 YEARS OLD INTERNET USAGE IN BRAZIL

29% Only 29% of them are monitored by their families

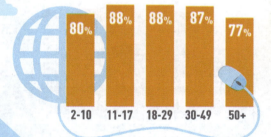

Unfortunately, there is danger online and it is important for both young users and adults to take precautions when using the internet. Families need to be cautious and aware of security, and should also monitor their children's internet use to prevent abuse or identity theft. Children and teenagers, on the other hand, need to be responsible and respect the limits established by their families for their own safety.

Based on: *Internet Facts*. <www.statista.com/search/?q=INTERNET+FACTS>; *Share of adults in the United States who use the internet*. Available at: <www.statista.com/statistics/266587/percentage-of-internet-users-by-age-groups/>; *Kids Safe Foundation*. Available at: <http://kidsafefoundation.org/>; *Online abuse: Facts and statistics*. Available at: <www.nspcc.org.uk/preventing-abuse/child-abuse-and-neglect/online-abuse/facts-statistics/>; T*he Senior's Guide to Online Safety*. Available at: <www.connectsafely.org/seniors/>; *As kids go online, identity theft claims more victims*. Available at: <www.cnbc.com/id/44583556>; *Pais devem acompanhar o acesso de crianças à internet, alertam especialistas*. Available at: <http://agenciabrasil.ebc.com.br/geral/noticia/2017-07/pais-devem-acompanhar-o-acesso-de-criancas-internet-alertam-especialistas>; *15 Facts about internet safety for parents*. Available at: <https://safety.lovetoknow.com/15_Facts_About_Internet_Safety>; *What are the dangers of using the web?* Available at: <www.affilorama.com/internet101/dangers-of-the-web>. Access: July 2018.

PROJECT

Ways to use internet safely

Work in groups and write a booklet that will work as an **Internet Safety Guide**. Your booklet should have:

- A cover;
- An introduction, explaining what virtual crime is, and the dangers people are exposed to when using the internet irresponsibly;
- Tips to help children and teens to protect themselves from virtual crimes.

Remember that your booklet will help kids and teens, so use lots of images, short texts, and tons of creativity!

Remember to have fun while creating it and use what you learned to protect yourself online!

FOCUS ON CULTURE II

GREENHOUSE EFFECT AND GLOBAL WARMING

The increase of Earth's surface and oceans average temperature has causes and effects.

PN: gases, like carbon dioxide, and methane, absorb heat that would otherwise bounce off the Earth's saurface, increasing the planet's temperature.

Agrotoxics, deforestation, greenhouse gases, and trash: the global average surface temperature rose 0.6 to 0.9 degrees Celsius (1.1 to 1.6° F) between 1906 and 2005.

Christiane S. Messias

Source: Global Climate Change - Vital Signs of the Planet. Available at: <https://climate.nasa.gov/>; Earth Observatory – Global Warming. Available at: <https://earthobservatory.nasa.gov/Features/GlobalWarming/page2.php>; What's your impact? Available at: <https://whatsyourimpact.org/greenhouse-effect>; Climate kids. Available at: <https://climatekids.nasa.gov/fossil-fuels-coal/>; World waste facts. Available at: <www.theworldcounts.com/counters/shocking_environmental_facts_and_statistics/world_waste_facts>; 35 Surprising facts about global warming. Available at: <www.conserve-energy-future.com/various-global-warming-facts.php>;

SAVE THE WORLD

PLANT A TREE
they produce oxygen and consume carbon dioxide

DO NOT BURN
recycle instead

SOLAR ENERGY
less than 1% of the world's energy source

RECYCLE
2.12 billion tons of waste globally each year

DEATHS
climate changes kill more than 400.000 people around the world per year

WASTE
99% of what we buy is trashed within 6 months

DO NOT CUT TREES
they can help

USE A BIKE
reduces the production of greenhouse gases

Christiane S. Messias

What causes global warming? Available at: <www.thoughtco.com/the-causes-of-global-warming-1203786>; Can you reduce greenhouse gas emissions? Available at: <www.thoughtco.com/reduce-greenhouse-gas-emissions-1203896>; Obama is right: Climate change kills more people than terrorism. Available at: <https://newrepublic.com/article/121032/map-climate-change-kills-more-people-worldwide-terrorism>. Access: July 2018.

PROJECT

Global Warming Awareness Campaign

In groups, develop an awareness campaign. The objective is to teach young children about the reasons and consequences of global warming. Think of efficient and simple ways of explaining its content to children. Discuss the following questions with your classmates:

- What will we do if we want to change this reality soon?
- What might happen if we don't stop global warming now?
- Could we use alternative energy sources? Which ones?
- What are the causes shown on the poster?
- What are the effects shown on the poster?
- What are the solutions shown on the poster?

When you are done, rehearse presenting your campaign to your classmates.

LANGUAGE COURT

||| Unit 1 |||

Page 11 and 12

The **simple future** tense (**will**) is used to talk about the future in general, when there is no plan or decision made upon it yet. It is more like a thought or a prediction about the future. It can be used together with verbs like *to guess* and *to think*, or adverbs like *probably*.

*I guess nobody **will** go to the beach if it keeps raining.*
*I think she **will** pass the final exams.*
*It **will** probably rain tomorrow.*

It can be used to suggest that a voluntarily action is being offered to someone else. Usually, it is used to make a request, to reply someone else's complaint or request or to decline something.

*I **will** send you the information when I get it.*
***Will** you help me move this heavy table?*
*I **will** not do your homework for you.*
A: *I'm really hungry.*
B: *I'll make some sandwiches.*

The **simple future** (**will**) is also used to express promises:

*I **will** call you when I arrive.*
*I promise I **will not** tell him about the surprise party.*

Now, look how it is formed:

Affirmative

Subject	Auxiliary verb (will)	Verb (infinitive)
I		participate.
He, she, it	will ('ll)	study.
We, you, they		visit.

*I **will** (I'll) help them with the packages.*
*She **will** (she'll) get a good grade on the math test.*
*They **will** (they'll) probably travel to Asia next month.*

Negative

Subject	Auxiliary verb	Negative (not)	Verb (infinitive)
I			participate.
He, she, it	will not (won't)		study.
We, you, they			visit.

*I **will not** (**won't**) help them with the packages.*
*She **will not** (**won't**) get a good grade on the math test.*
*They **will not** (**won't**) probably travel to Asia next month.*

Interrogative

Auxiliary verb (will)	Subject	Verb (infinitive)	Rest of the sentence
			the poor?
Will	I he, she, it we, you, they	help study visit	for the exams?
			our parents next holiday?

***Will** you help them with the packages?*
***Will** she get a good grade on the math test?*
***Will** they travel to Asia next month?*

Page 14

A conjunction is a part of the speech used to connect words, phrases, clauses, or sentences. They allow to form complex, elegant sentences and avoid the choppiness of multiple short sentences.

There are several types of conjunctions that accomplish various functions within the sentence. They can be:

- **Coordinating**: allow you to join words, phrases, and clauses of equal grammatical rank in a sentence.
- **Correlative**: are pairs of conjunctions that work together.
- **Subordinating**: join independent and dependent clauses; it can signal a cause-and-effect relationship, a contrast, or some other kind of relationship between the clauses.
- **Conjunctive adverb**: always connects one clause to another, and is used to show sequence, contrast, cause and effect, and other relationships.

There are a few important rules for using conjunctions:

- They are for connecting thoughts, actions, and ideas as well as nouns, clauses, and other parts of speech.
- They are useful for making lists.
- When using conjunctions, make sure that all the parts of the sentences agree.

Now, take a look at four of the most common conjunctions used in American English.

- **Because** (subordinating): expresses the reason for something.
  *I can go to the field trip **because** I got good grades this semester.*

- **So** (coordinating): expresses the result of something.
  *Jesse didn't have much money, **so** she gave up on buying a new dress.*

- **If** (subordinating): expresses an assumption or condition to something to happen.
  *I can help you **if** you pay me first.*

- **Then** (conjunctive adverb): expresses a consequence or result of something.
  *First, Mark bought a house, **then** he got married.*

||| Unit 2 |||

Page 25 to 27

The **simple future** tense (**be going to**) is used to talk about the future when there is already a plan or a decision previously made upon it.

*I'**m going to** buy some milk, once we ran out of it.*
*She **is going to** travel today, because the fares are low now.*

It can be used to make a prediction about the future, once there is evidence for that in the present.

*Look at those boys playing football! They'**re going to** break the window.*
*The sky is getting darker and darker. It'**s going to** rain.*

Now, look how it is formed:

Affirmative

Subject	Auxiliary verb (to be)	Auxiliary verb (going to)	Verb (infinitive)
I	am		participate. study. visit.
He, she, it	is	going to	
We, you, they	are		

*I **am** (I'**m**) **going to** help them today.*
*She **is** (she'**s**) **going to** get a good seat at the stadium.*
*They **are** (they'**re**) **going to** travel to Asia next month.*

Negative

Subject	Auxiliary verb (to be)	Negative (not)	Auxiliary verb (going to)	Verb (infinitive)
I	am	not ('m not)		participate. study. visit.
He, she, it	is	not (isn't)	going to	
We, you, they	are	not (aren't)		

*I **am not** (**'m not**) **going to** help them with the packages.*
*She **is not** (**isn't**) **going to** get a good grade on the math test.*
*They **are not** (**aren't**) **going to** travel to Asia next month.*

Interrogative

Auxiliary verb (be)	Subject	Auxiliary verb (going to)	Verb (infinitive)
Am	I		help? study? visit?
Is	he, she, it	going to	
Are	we, you, they		

***Are** you **going to** help them with the packages?*
***Is** she **going to** get a good grade on the math test?*
***Are** they **going to** travel to Asia next month?*

||| Unit 3 |||

Page 43

An **embedded question** is a question in another question. In other words, it is a question that appears in a **declarative statement** or **in another question**. They are very common after introductory phrases, such as:

- *I wonder.*
- *Could you tell me.*
- *Do you know.*
- *Can you remember.*
- *Let's ask.*
- *We need to find out.*
- *I'd like to know.*
- *Could you tell me.*
- *I'm not sure.*
- *Would you mind explaining.*

Unlike conventional interrogative structures, in which word order is reversed, the subject usually comes before the verb in an embedded question. Take a look:

Direct Question	Embedded Question
Where can I find the information booth?	Do you know where I can find the information booth?
Where do I get a cab?	Can you tell me where I get a cab?
How much does the ticket cost?	Could you tell me how much the ticket costs?
What time does the Mingles Pub open?	Would you tell me what time the Mingles Pub opens?
How far is the Mingles Pub?	Can you tell me how far the Mingles Pub is?

There are rules for using embedded questions:
- If it is part of a **statement**, use a period and not a question mark at the end of the sentence. Also, if is in the **simple present** or **simple past**, omit the auxiliary verbs and change the verb to its appropriate form.

Direct Question	Embedded Question
What time **did** he **leave**?	I wonder what time he **left**.

- If it includes an **auxiliary verb** or the verb **to be**, reverse the positions of the subject and the auxiliary verb.

Direct Question	Embedded Question
What **did he** say?	Could you tell me what **he said**?
Is he a doctor?	Do you know if **he is** a doctor?

- Do not use a verbal contraction at the end of the sentence.

Direct Question	**Correct** Embedded Question	**Incorrect** Embedded Question
Where **is he**?	Do you know where **he is**?	Do you know where **he's**?

- They are introduced by **whether**, **whether**, or **not**, and **if** when there is no question word in the sentence (yes/no questions).

Direct Yes/No Question	Embedded Question
Will he be there?	Do you know **if** he will be there?
	Do you know **whether or not** he will be there?
	Do you know **whether** he will be there or not?

- The infinitive can follow a **question word** or **whether** in embedded questions:

Direct Question	Embedded Question	Embedded Question with an Infinitive
What should I do?	Please tell me what I should do.	Please tell me what to do.

- There are two scenarios when native English speakers prefer to use embedded rather than direct questions:

To politely ask for information:

Direct Question	Embedded Question
What time does the bus arrive?	Could you tell me what time the bus arrives? (more polite)

To talk about something unknown to the speaker:

Direct Question	Embedded Question
Why did she decide not to come with us?	I don't know why she decided not to come with us.

Page 45

The simple future (will) indicates probability in the future, when you are not sure about it. It's when you decide to do something at the time of speaking; it is not a previous decision, it is mainly a new idea.

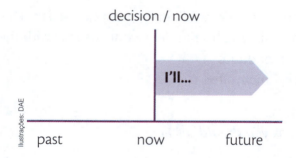

The simple future (be going to) indicates concrete plans for the future, when you are sure about them; it is about something you have already decided to do.

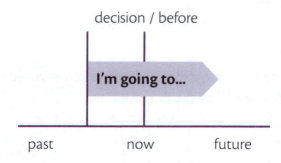

Take a look at the differences:

Will / won't + verb	Be going to + verb
I guess **I'll find** a summer job.	**I'm going to take care** of my little brother.
He probably **won't let** me go to the party.	**I'm not going to go** to the party.
I think **I'll see** you next year.	What **are you going to do?**

||| Unit 4 |||

Page 57 and 58

Modal verbs are auxiliary verbs that express necessity or possibility. They are used to express an idea that is not expressed by the main verb.

The modal verb **should / should not** (**shouldn't**) is used to give advice or to talk about what we think right or wrong. It is used to express the opinion of a speaker and often follows *I think* **or** *I don't think*. It is less formal, and it is used to give advice.

> *You look tired. I think you **should** take a few days off.*
> *Alice works for long hours. She **should** talk to her boss.*
> *Nancy looks sleepy. I think she **shouldn't** drive.*
> *Peter played for long hours. He **shouldn't** do that so often.*
> ***Should** I wear a tie?*
> *What **should** I wear tonight?*

This modal has many uses that do not fit easily into one pattern. The best way to approach this word is to take note of each use as you hear it. Here we are dealing with the following meanings:

- Talking about obligation or duties:
  *He **should** see his mother more often.*

- Asking for / Giving advice:
  *What **should** I do? I think you **should** call her.*

The modal verb **had better** is used to give advice in the present or future and in specific situations, not general ones. When we use had better, there is a suggestion that, if the advice is not followed, something bad will happen. It implies a negative consequence.

> *You **had better** tell her everything.*
> *She **had better** do what I say or else she will get into trouble.*
> *You**'d better** not be late.*

The modal verb **ought to** is the most formal of the structures used for giving advice, that's why it isn't so common. It is always followed by the preposition to.

*You **ought to** contact the police.*
*You **ought not to** cheat in exams.*
*You **ought not to** wear black shoes.*

Pay attention: the modals **had better** and **ought to** are not commonly used in questions.

The modal verb **must** often expresses obligations that the speaker feels like necessary. In the present tense, it takes the same form in all persons and it is followed by the verb in the infinitive form.

*I **must** obey the school rules.*
*He **must** obey his parents.*
*They **must** obey the law like everybody else.*

On the other hand, the modal verb **mustn't** expresses that something is prohibited.

*I **mustn't** talk to strangers on the street.*
*You **mustn't** answer telephone calls from strangers.*

The modal verb **have to** is used to express obligations that come from an external source such as another person or organization. It is like a rule that we are required to follow. As is the present tense, **have to** takes the same form in all persons, but it becomes **has to** in the 3rd person singular.

*You **have to** go to the party.*
*He **has to** call her.*

The negative form of this modal verb (**don't have to / doesn't have to**) expresses that something is not required.

*You **don't have** to wear a tie.*
*He **doesn't have to** worry about it.*

The modal verb **need to** expresses necessity to do something, i.e., that something is necessary, but not obligatory.

*I **need to** go home to help dad with dinner.*
*You **need to** sleep early today because you have a math test tomorrow morning.*

The negative form of this modal verb (**don't need to / doesn't need to**) expresses that something is not necessary.

*You **don't need to** bring food.*
*He **doesn't need to** wear a suit.*

||| Unit 5 |||

Page 75 to 77

We use the **past perfect tense** to show that an action happened before another past event.

We were shocked that someone **had graffitied** the school wall.

We also use the **past perfect** when we want to mention a point in the past and there is the need to refer to an event that occurred before it. This allows us to clearly show the sequence of the events in a more specific way.

If I had woken up earlier this morning, I would have got in class on time.

Now, look how it is formed:

Affirmative

Subject pronoun	Auxiliary verb (present tense had)	Main verb (past participle)
I He / She / It You / We / They	had	done. made. slept. woken up.

*The train **had left** when he arrived at the station.*
*They **had put** the washing out when it started to rain.*

Negative

Subject pronoun	Auxiliary verb (present tense had)	Negative (not)	Main verb (past participle)
I He / She / It You / We / They	had	not (hadn't)	done. made. slept. woken up.

*The train **had not** (**hadn't**) **left** when he arrived at the station.*
*They **had not** (**hadn't**) **put** the washing out when it started to rain.*

Interrogative

Auxiliary verb (present tense had)	Subject pronoun	Main verb (past participle)
Had	I he / she / it you / we / they	done? made? slept? woken up?

***Had** the train **left** when he arrived at the station?*
***Had** they **put** the washing out when it started to rain?*

||| Unit 6 |||

Page 89 to 91

The **passive voice** is used when we want to emphasize the action (the verb) and the object of a sentence rather than subject. This means that the subject is either less important than the action itself or that we don't know who or what the subject is. Take a look:

Active voice	Passive voice
Someone **stole** my laptop.	My laptop **was stolen**.
Someone **killed** twenty civilians in the bomb explosion.	Twenty civilians **were killed** in the bomb explosion.

In the **passive voice**, the agent of the passive can be identified **at the end of the sentence** and preceded with the preposition **by**.

Mona Lisa was painted **by Leonardo da Vinci.**

Most of the time, writing experts recommend against using the passive voice, when possible, once using the active voice makes the writing clearer and less complicated. The passive is often used to report something or to state a fact.

Highway 20 **was closed** *yesterday due to a serious road accident.*
A lot of flowers **are grown** *in Holambra.*

Now, look how it is formed:

Affirmative

Subject pronoun	Auxiliary verb (to be)	Main verb (past participle)
I He / She / It You / We / They	am / is / are am / is / are + being was / were was / were + being will + be am / is / are + going to be have / has + been had + been will have + been can / could + be have / has to + be must + be	done. made. slept. woken up.

Many films **are made** *in India.*
The e-mail **is being sent** *at this moment.*

*The president **was invited** to make a speech.*
*The dishes **were being washed** when their parents arrived home.*
*A new government plan **will be discussed** next month.*
*A technical school **is going to be built** in a near future in town.*
*That company **has been sold** for a very large sum of money.*
*All the workers **had been informed** about the situation of the company.*
*By next month, a new mayor **will have been elected**.*
*This shampoo **can be** easily **found** in the supermarket.*
*A new salesman **has to be hired** this week.*
*Those books **must be read** by the end of this month.*

Negative

Subject pronoun	Auxiliary verb (to be)	Negative (not)	Main verb (past participle)
I He / She / It You / We / They	am / is / are **not** am / is / are **not** + being was / were **not** was / were **not** + being will **not** + be am / is / are **not** + going to be have / has **not** + been had **not** + been will **not** have + been can / could **not** + be do **not** have to / does **not** have to + be must **not** + be do **not** + have to		done. made. slept. woken up.

*Many films **aren't made** in India.*
*The e-mail **isn't being sent** at this moment.*
*The president **wasn't invited** to make a speech.*
*The dishes **weren't being washed** when their parents arrived home.*
*A new government plan **won't be discussed** next month.*
*A technical school **isn't going to be built** in a near future in town.*
*That company **hasn't been sold** for a very large sum of money.*
*All the workers **hadn't been informed** about the situation of the company.*
*By next month, a new mayor **will not have been elected**.*
*This shampoo **can't be** easily **found** in the supermarket.*
*A new salesman **doesn't have to be hired** this week.*
*Those books **mustn't be read** by the end of this month.*

Interrogative

Auxiliary verb (to be)	Subject pronoun	Auxiliary verb	Main verb (past participle)
Am / Is / Are Was / Were Will Have / Has Had Will have Can / Could Have / Has to Must	I he / she / it you / we / they	being be going to be been be	done? made? slept? woken up?

Are many films **made** in India?
Is the e-mail **being sent** at this moment?
Was the president **invited** to make a speech?
Were the dishes **being washed** when their parents arrived home?
Will a new government plan **be discussed** next month?
Is a technical school **going to be built** in a near future in town?
Has that company **been sold** for a very large sum of money?
Had all the workers **been informed** about the situation of the company?
Will a new mayor **have been elected** by next month?
Can this shampoo **be** easily **found** in the supermarket?
Does a new salesman **have to be hired** this week?
Must those books **be read** by the end of the month?

||| Unit 7 |||

Page 107 to 109

The **first conditional** is used to talk about things which might happen in the future. It is used to describe possible things, which could easily come true.

If it rains, I won't go to the park.
If I study today, I'll go to the party tonight.
If I have enough money, I'll buy some new shoes.

The conditional is formed by two parts: the if-clause, that shows the condition to something to happen, and the main clause that shows the "result".

In the first conditional, the if-clause is always in the simple present tense, and the main clause, in the simple future. Take a look at its structure:

If-clause			Main clause			
If	subject pronoun	simple present		subject pronoun	simple future (will)	main verb (infinitive)	
If	you	read	a lot,	you	will	improve	your writing.
If	he	doesn't sleep	enough,	he	will	get	tired.
If	they	eat	too much sugar,	they	won't	be	healthy.

If they do not pass their exam, they will not go to college.
If we do not earn enough, we will not travel on our vacation.
Jane will be happy if you help her.
If it rains tomorrow, will you read that book?
What will you say if you meet them?
Where will Mary live if she gets her new job?

||| Unit 8 |||

Page 121

The **second conditional** is used to talk about unreal situations. It describes hypothetical possibilities for a particular condition and its most probable result.

If I had a million dollars, I would buy a big house.
If I won the lottery, I would buy a car.
I would travel the world if I had a million dollars.

The conditional is formed by two parts: the if-clause, that shows the condition to something to happen, and the main clause that shows the "result". Usually the if-clause comes first and a comma is used. When the if-clause comes second, there is no need for a comma.

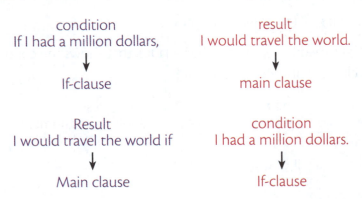

In the **second conditional**, the if-clause is always in the simple past tense, and the main clause uses auxiliary or modal verbs: would, could or might. Take a look at its structure:

	If-clause			Main clause			
If	subject pronoun	simple past		subject pronoun	modal verb	main verb (infinitive)	
If	I	were	you,	I	would	sleep	more.
If	Jane	repaired	the old taps,	she	could	save	water.
If	they	rode	their bikes to school,	they	might	get	there late.

I'd go to the movies with you if I didn't have to study for the English test.
If I had a car, I would invite you to go to the beach.
If Jane spoke French better, she could be a bilingual secretary.
What would you do if you found a wallet on the street?
If I had more money, I could buy a new computer.
If they studied harder, they might pass the examination.

Note that this simple past form is slightly different from the usual in the case of the verb to be. Whatever the subject, in the second conditional, the verb form is always **were**:

*If **I were** rich, I'd buy a big house.*
*If **she were** rich, she'd buy a big house.*
*If **they were** rich, they'd buy a big house.*

Page 122

The **third conditional** is used to talk about unreal situations regarding the past. It describes hypothetical possibilities for a particular condition in the past that did not happen, it is an impossible past condition.

If she had studied, she would have passed the exam.
If I hadn't eaten so much, I wouldn't have felt sick.
If we had taken a taxi, we wouldn't have missed the plane.

The conditional is formed by two parts: the if-clause, that shows the condition to something to happen, and the main clause that shows the "result".

In the **third conditional** the if-clause is always in the **past perfect tense**, and the main clause uses would + present perfect. Take a look at how it is formed:

	If-clause			Main clause			
If	**subject pronoun**	**past perfect**		**subject pronoun**	**modal verb**	**present perfect**	
If	I	had won	the lottery,	I	would	have travelled	more.
If	Jane	hadn't eaten	so much,	she	wouldn't	have felt	sick.
If	they	had been	free yesterday,	they	would	have gone	to the movies.

If she had been more careful, she wouldn't have broken the glass.
If she had seen him, she would have said hello.
If he had looked at me, I would have smiled at him.
She would have died if the doctor hadn't arrived quickly.
I would have gone to your graduation party if I hadn't been busy.
The volleyball team would have lost if the players hadn't performed well.
She wouldn't have fallen in love if he had been a jealous man.

GLOSSARY

A

abroad: fora
accommodation: acomodação
acculturation: aculturação
acknowledgment: reconhecimento
acre: acre (unidade de medida de área)
affordability: acessibilidade
AFK (away from the keyboard): longe do teclado
airplane: avião
allow: permitir
ambulance: ambulância
amusement: divertimento
ancient: antigo
angry: bravo
antivirus: antivírus
apply: aplicar
ASAP (as soon as possible): o mais cedo possível
assemble: montar
assume: assumir
astray: desviar
attempt: tentativa

B

background: plano de fundo; experiência prévia
backup: apoio; cópia de segurança; apoiar; fazer cópias
bag: bolsa, sacola
bang: bater
based: baseado
battery: bateria
beach: praia
because: porque (resposta)
belief: crença
bias: viés, distorção de julgamento.
big: grande

bike: bicicleta
bin: lixeira
blindman's buff: cabra-cega
boar: javali
boil off: ferver, evaporar
book (verb): reservar
bored: entediado
boring: entediante
bottle: garrafa
BRB (be right back): volto já
bus: ônibus
buy: comprar

C

come out of: sair de algum lugar
camera: câmera
canoe: canoa
capture the flag: rouba bandeira
car: carro
car-boot sale: forma de mercado em que as pessoas se reúnem para vender produtos domésticos e artigos de jardinagem que são colocados no porta-malas (boot) dos automóveis
carriage: carruagem
carry out: executar
casing: revestimento; invólucro
chat room: sala de bate-papo
cheap: barato
chilling: assustador
choice: escolha
clay: argila
cloth: tecido; pano
clothing: vestimenta
college: faculdade
comfortable: confortável
compost bin: depósito de compostagem

confused: confuso
conscientious: consciente
container: contêiner
convenient: conveniente
convey: transmitir
creature: criatura
crop: safra
crossroad: encruzilhada
current: atual
cut out: cortar
decision making: tomada de decisão

D

decode: decodificar
definitely: definitivamente
deplete: esgotar
devour: devorar
digital music player: tocador de música digital
dinner: jantar
disability: incapacidade; deficiência
displace: deslocar
displaced: deslocado
disruption: interrupção
dozens: dezenas (informal)
dugout: abrigo

E

electric energy: energia elétrica
embarrassed: envergonhado
endure: suportar
engine: motor
enjoyable: gratificante, agradável
ensure: garantir
entangled: emaranhado
entertainment: entretenimento
entrepreneurial: empreendedor
excited: animado
expensive: caro
exploitation: exploração

F

face-to-face: cara a cara
face with: defrontar-se com
fairly: justamente
fast: rápido
fear: medo
feature: apresentar
ferry boat: balsa
figure: figura
finite: limitado, finito
fly a kite: empinar pipa
forecast: prever
format: formatar
fossil fuel: combustível fóssil
foster care: sistema de acolhimento
freeze tag: variação da brincadeira pega-pega
funny: engraçado

G

gas lamp: lampião
gear: equipar
gender: gênero
geological: geológico
get married: casar-se
ghost in the graveyard: variação da brincadeira esconde-esconde
glider: planador
go off: sair; explodir; disparar
go shopping: fazer compras
god-like: divino
graduate: formar-se
gramophone: gramofone
grant: conceder
ground-breaking: inovador
groundwater: água subterrânea
grown-up: adulto

H

hack into: invadir; hackear, raquear
hand-clap: palmas, aplauso
happy: feliz
haptic: tátil
harm: prejudicar
hasty: apressado
hazardous: perigoso
hazy: nebuloso
health care: sistema de saúde
health insurance: seguro--saúde
heap: grande quantidade
heavy: pesado
helicopter: helicóptero
hide and seek: esconde--esconde
high hopes: grandes esperanças (expectativas)
high school: ensino médio
hobbyhorse: cavalinho de madeira
hollow-out: tornar oco
hometown: cidade natal
hopscotch: amarelinha (brincadeira infantil)
host of metals: variedade de metais
hostel: albergue
hot-air balloon: balão de ar quente
housework: trabalho doméstico
hula-hoop: bambolê
hybrid: híbrido

I

IDK (I don't know): eu não sei
IMO (In my opinion): na minha opinião
in love: apaixonado

increasingly besieged: aumentado o assédio
infotainment: entretenimento informativo
infuse: infundir, inspirar
instant message: mensagem instantânea

J

jar: vaso; jarra
jigsaw puzzle: quebra-cabeças
job: trabalho
jump-rope: pular corda

K

keep up: acompanhar, manter
kick the can: variação da brincadeira pega-pega
kidnap: sequestrar
kidnapping: sequestro

L

laid back: descontraído
lamp bulb: lâmpada incandescente
laptop: computador portátil
latest: mais recente
launch: lançar
laundry: lavandeira
law: direito, lei
lead to: levar a
leak: vazar
leftover: sobra de comida
letter: carta
light: luz
liquid-fueled: abastecido por líquido
lizard: lagarto
load: carga
log: registro

LOL (laughing out loud): rindo muito alto
loom: aproximar-se
lumber: tábua de madeira

M

mail: correspondência
manned: tripulado
manner: maneira
manufacture: fabricar
manufactured: fabricado
marbles: bolinha de gude
mass-produced: produzido em massa
means of communication: meios de comunicação
merchandise: negociar
mindful: atento
miscommunication: falta de comunicação
mistreated: maltratado
misunderstanding: mal--entendido
money: dinheiro
motorbike: motocicleta
myth: mito
mythological: mitológico

N

napkin: guardanapo
near: aproximar-se
neurohack: hackear (raquear) o cérebro
newspaper: jornal

O

OMG (Oh my God): Ai meu Deus (expressão)
on foot: a pé
on the other hand: por outro lado

onwards: em diante
ore: minério
otherwise: de outra forma
outpace: ultrapassar
output: produção
overnight: durante a noite

P

packaging: embalagem
pastime: passatempo
pavement: pavimento
PDA (Personal Digital Assistant): assistente pessoal digital
peaceful: calmo; pacífico
perceive: perceber
peril: perigo
perovskite: perovskita (mineral relativamente raro)
pet: animal de estimação
photon: fóton (partícula elementar mediadora da força eletromagnética)
picnic: piquenique, fazer piquenique
plan out: planejar
plastic: plástico
plaything: brinquedo
portable: portátil
prediction: previsão
prescription drug: remédio prescrito
prevail: prevalecer
probably: provavelmente
produce: produzir
pursue: buscar, ir atrás de

R

rail line: linha de trem
raw material: matéria-prima
rec'd (abbreviation of received): recebido

reckless: imprudente
recognized: reconhecido
refugee: refugiado
release: lançamento
replenish: reabastecer
reproduced: reproduzido
repurpose: reaproveitar, reutilizar
research: pesquisar
reset: restabelecer, recompor
resolute: resoluto
resource: fonte, recurso
responsibility: responsabilidade
reusable: reutilizável
rocket: foguete
ROLFT (rolling on the floor laughing): rolando de rir no chão
rubbish: lixo
run out of: acabar, esgotar

S

sad: triste
sail boat: barco a vela
savvy: esclarecido
scrap paper: papel de rascunho
script: roteiro
seek: procurar
selfless: altruísta
self-propelled: autopropelido
self-reliant: autossuficiente
sell: vender
sensible: sensato
set up: configurar
setting: cenário
shake up: sacudir
shaky: instável
sheet: folha (de papel); lençol
shift: mudança
ship: navio
sightseeing: passeio

sled: trenó
sleepy: sonolento
slow: lento
small: pequeno
social networking site: rede social
souvenir: lembrancinha
span: período
speed boat: lancha
stand: parar
standard: padrão
steam engine: motor a vapor
steamboat: barco a vapor
stick with: aderir
strip out: esvaziar
subway: metrô
summary: resumo
supply: fornecimento
surprised: surpreso
swift: rápido; veloz

T

tag: rotular; marcar
take back: pegar de volta
take into account: levar em consideração
technician: técnico
teetotum: piorra (pião)
telecom: telecomunicação
threatening: ameaçador

thrilled to death: muito satisfeito e animado (expressão idiomática)
ticket: bilhete, passagem
timeless: eterno; atemporal
tip: dica
tiring: cansativo
to be raised: ser criado
to overrun: devastar
train: trem
trend: tendência
trick: trapaça, truque; trapacear; enganar
trouble: problema
truck: caminhão
TV set: aparelho de televisão
type up: digitar
typewriter: máquina de escrever

U

undecisive: indeciso
unfairly: injustamente
unfixed: sem fixação
unhackable: não pode ser hackeado (raqueado)
upon: sobre
use: usar
user-friendly: simples, intuitivo, acessível

V

valuable: valioso
video chat: vídeo chamada
VoIP (Voice over Internet Protocol): VoIP (voz sobre protocolo de Internet)

W

wagon: carroça; vagão
warn: avisar
wasteful: desperdício
western: ocidental
whether: se
why: por que (pergunta)
wide: vasto
widely: amplamente
work out: definir; elaborar
workforce: força de trabalho, trabalhadores
wrap up: embrulhar
wrath: ira

Y

youth: juventude